A SERIES OF UNRELATED EVENTS

A SERIES OF UNRELATED EVENTS

Richard Bacon

CENTURY

Published by Century 2013

2 4 6 8 10 9 7 5 3 1

Copyright © Richard Bacon 2013

Richard Bacon has asserted his right under the Copyright, Designs
and Patents Act 1988 to be identified as the author of this work

This book is a work of non-fiction based on the life, experiences and recollections
of the author. In some limited cases names of people, places, dates, sequences
or the details of events have been changed to protect the privacy of others. The
author has stated to the publishers that, except in such minor respects not affecting
the substantial accuracy of the work, the contents of this book are true.

First published in Great Britain in 2013 by
Century
Random House, 20 Vauxhall Bridge Road,
London SW1V 2SA

www.randomhouse.co.uk

Addresses for companies within The Random House Group Limited can
be found at: www.randomhouse.co.uk

The Random House Group Limited Reg. No. 954009

A CIP catalogue record for this book
is available from the British Library

ISBN 9781780890562

The Random House Group Limited supports the Forest Stewardship Council®
(FSC®), the leading international forest-certification organisation.
Our books carrying the FSC® label are printed on FSC®-certified paper.
FSC® is the only forest-certification scheme supported by the
leading environmental organisations, including Greenpeace.
Our paper procurement policy can be found at:
www.randomhouse.co.uk/environment

Printed and bound by CPI Group (UK) Ltd, Croydon, CR0 4YY

For Arthur[1]

---

[1] Arthur, please don't read this book.

CONTENTS

A SERIES OF UNRELATED EVENTS

Chapter 1

COCAINE, AND LOTS OF IT

I've been trying to remember the details of the evening that took me from being a successful children's television presenter that nobody had heard of to an unsuccessful children's television presenter that everybody had heard of.

I can't recall all the details of those forty-eight hours and you don't really need to hear them. I'll give you the start and end points and I reckon you can join the dots of decline.

It began at 6 p.m. in the picturesque White Cross Inn by the river in leafy Richmond, where I supped a pint of Theakstons Old Peculier as the sun set over Old Father Thames.

It ended at 8 a.m. in a frightening drug dealer's flat in Tottenham.

It's so long ago and I was in such a state that the murky stuff between those two points really is hazy. But I can recall being in that drug dealer's flat. I didn't know him. I didn't even know the person who had taken me there. But I do remember that as I walked through the door he recognised me as 'Hey, aren't you that dude from *Blue Peter*?'

And that right there may have been the bleakest moment in my life.

It was three weeks later that the *News of the World* (RIP) ran the story of that romantic evening. They sat on it, waiting so the piece coincided with *Blue Peter*'s fortieth anniversary celebrations.

The BBC took those celebrations seriously. A mammoth party was thrown in the show's honour at London's Natural History Museum. (I mean the party was big, it didn't specifically involve the mammoth.) All of the living presenters, past and present, were there, although one of the present was about to become one of the past.

Two things stick in my mind from that bash. One: meeting my hero and childhood fantasy figure Caron Keating and two: leaving – making my way past the diplodocus, through the grand doorway, down the steps and into the path of a pair of single-minded, somewhat sinister-looking paparazzi photographers.

Initially this rather flattered my ego. But then I noticed something curious – the determined lads were focusing all of their attention on me and completely ignoring the better-known *Blue Peter* hosts.

I let that worry slide.

Oh, I thought, these guys know a rising star when they see one. I half recall one of my colleagues whispering to me 'You've arrived.'

Anthea Turner was, back then, perhaps the biggest name on television, hosting *GMTV*, *The National Lottery* and *Wish You Were Here* (all RIP). She had just got divorced and her new fella had left his wife for her. She was one hundred per cent tabloid fodder. And yet . . . when she walked past that diplodocus, through the grand doorway and down the steps, the cameras remained focused on yours truly.

I now *knew* something wasn't right. And although I didn't realise it at that point, I had indeed 'arrived', because in a matter of hours I would become a household name, provided that household took the *News of the World*.

Such was my dopey decision-making capacity that this creeping sense of *something-not-being-right* didn't stop me – completely failed to stop me – from going *straight* to the Ministry of Sound nightclub in Elephant and Castle (not nice). I left at 6 a.m. On the way out a stranger stopped to tell me, 'There's a couple of photographers waiting outside for you.'

I still find those words haunting.

Because at that point, really, I knew it was all over.

Not in such simple terms. I didn't consciously think 'That's it, my career's done.' But I was hit by a sense of impending doom.

As I stepped out of the Ministry of Sound it was raining, it was dark, I looked a mess, it was 6 a.m., I was in Elephant and Castle and the same two photographers were snapping and flashing relentlessly and aggressively in my face.

I asked one of them, 'Why are you following me?'

He said, almost a bit regretfully, 'We can't tell you.'

So now I know that I've been targeted by newspaper photographers who've been sworn to secrecy.

When you leave nightclubs like that at six in the morning, you are not short on feelings of anxiety and paranoia. Now imagine a man with a camera comes up to you and essentially says, 'I've been following you for the entire night and I can't tell you why.' That was probably the second bleakest moment of my life.

The following morning (by which I mean the same morning, but after I'd gone home, lain on the bed for two hours, not slept and had a shower) was a Saturday. I called my agent, Jon Holmes, to tell him about the photographers who'd been tailing me.

He didn't like the sound of it and put me on to the agency's media advisor, Stuart Higgins, a recently departed editor of *The Sun* newspaper.

'Following you around all evening?' he said. 'That's very strange. I'll ring round and call you right back.'

The next person I telephoned was my best friend. Coincidentally, he'd been out with me on *that* night (you know, the one that started in leafy Richmond and ended up . . .). He'd been my 'wingman'. He reassured me, saying it would be alright and telling me I was probably worrying over nothing. He even ventured to flatter me a little, saying I was a rising star so why *wouldn't* the press be interested in me?

I informed him that the super competent Stuart Higgins

was on my case, so that was *some* good news.

I was living at the time in a small two-bedroom flat in West London's Chiswick. I'd only just moved in and the previous owners had painted the hallway yellow. Obviously, that had to go. And this was the day that I had arranged for my upstanding criminal defence solicitor father, Paul, to come down from Mansfield and help me redecorate.

Now, understand this. My parents are deeply middle-class and live in a relatively small town. And when your parents are deeply middle-class and live in a relatively small town, having a son on *Blue Peter* is the biggest deal. To them, there is no other show I could ever present that would come remotely close to that level of prestige. Even if I were to front the BBC's coverage of the coronation of King Charles (trivia fans, he'll actually be called King George VII), my mum would say, 'Yeah, that's nice, but it's no *Blue Peter*.'

For my first ever programme they gathered all of their friends around our living-room television. There was Kirit, the local doctor, Andy, the jeweller, John, the bathroom showroom owner, and Heather, the local councillor.

They sipped champagne (actually, it was probably prosecco) and watched excitedly as Katy Hill decorated me with my official *Blue Peter* badge before I introduced a report in which I drove a floating Ferrari around a lake at Longleat.

This was, I suspect, the happiest my parents have ever been (and I'm including the births of myself and my sisters Helena and Juliet in that consideration).

So there me and my parents were, cock of the walk, living right at the summit of middle-class existence – and the problem with being on a towering summit is that there's only one way to go.

As my dad arrived at my flat that grim morning, I knew I had started to fall. I just wasn't aware at what velocity.

But nothing had been confirmed. Not yet. I didn't want to alarm my dad unduly.

So as scheduled, Dad and I went to the Kew branch of Homebase to pick out the paint. I still remember the one I went for. Midnight Mist.

As we travelled back along the A316, I was feeling sick. I couldn't concentrate on my father's conversation. I'm terrible at dealing with uncertainty, especially when I *know* I've done something wrong.

The tin of Midnight Mist was by my feet, the phone I kept turning over and over in my right hand.

Two minutes from home . . . it rang.

'Hello?'

'Richard, it's Stuart Higgins. Can you talk?'

'Not really,' I said sheepishly, while glancing over at my dad, Paul Bacon, the respected defence solicitor (and chairman of Mansfield Round Table). 'What have you found out?'

This is not an approximation. These are the exact words Stuart Higgins used.

'It's *News of the World*, cocaine and *lots of it*. Call me when you can talk.'

I knew two things in that instant: I was going to lose my job and I was going to break my dad's heart.

When we were back at the flat, I walked into the living room, Dad clutching the can of Midnight Mist – now a trivial purchase that mocked the gravity of what I was about to tell him.

I explained that I was going to be in the newspaper because of a story. Then I told him what that story was about.

'Is it true?' he asked. I said it was.

I simply can't remember what he said next. I don't particularly want to. I can only give you a broad outline. He became very intense and wanted to know if there was any way of stopping it getting into the paper. I told him probably not. He called my mum. She was upset, but, in a complete reversal of my parents' normal roles, she remained reasonably calm and rational.

Stuart Higgins called me again, an excuse for me to get out of the flat.

He had something of a bombshell. A thriller-like twist.

'The person who's done this to you,' he said, 'you've spoken to them today.'

I'd spoken to five people that day. Stuart Higgins, my dad, my mum and my best friend. And the paint specialist at the Kew branch of Homebase.

By a process of elimination, it came down to my best friend and the paint specialist at the Kew branch of Homebase. And it wasn't the paint specialist at the Kew branch of Homebase.

I now found myself with a lot to take in. I was going to lose my job. I was about to be all over the news. I'd devastated my parents. My hall was going to remain yellow for longer than planned. And I had been betrayed by my best friend.

They say you can't put a price on friendship – well, he did. Twenty grand.

Two minutes after Stuart had told me this unsettling news, my little pal called. You might think that a natural reaction would be to start bawling at him, but I had a surprisingly clear head. I stared at the handset, his name flashing on the screen, and made a calm, rational decision – to play the long game.

So I strung him along. I updated him and told him there was going to be a bad story about me in the newspaper, to which he replied, 'I hope you know that it's got nothing to do with me.' I reassured him: 'Of course not. You're my best friend.'

Let me now fill you in on what my best bud had been up to between *that* night (you know, the one that started in leafy Richmond and ended . . .) and this moment.

Not too long after the (and I here quote the *News of the World*) 'twelve-hour vodka and cocaine binge' (actually, it was fourteen hours: a rare example of tabloid understatement) he'd got in touch with the paper to inform them of my night's, well *our* night's, misdemeanours. They told him they needed hard evidence and suggested he ring me up, rehash the details of the night in a conversation, get some choice admissions and record the entire thing.

Sort of phone hacking. But without the hacking bit.

I recalled, belatedly that a couple of days earlier we had, in fact, had a rather odd chat on the blower about that big night out.

'So Rich, how much do you reckon we got through that night?'

'Don't remember.'

'No, come on, think. Two wraps?'

'Er, yeah, maybe.'

'So that much then, right? Er, how many did I just say?'

'Yeah, I guess two wraps.'

This is why, when Stuart Higgins faxed through (it was 1998) the copy from the *News of the World* that Saturday afternoon, it explained why there was a word-for-word transcript of our conversation.

The editor of *Blue Peter* at the time was the amiable and (to use one of his own words) 'jolly' Oliver MacFarlane. It's always been one of TV's most prestigious jobs, made famous by Biddy Baxter – one of those names that anyone who watched kids' TV during the 1970s and 1980s will instantly recognise without quite knowing why.

Biddy was a visionary producer, having introduced the *Blue Peter* badge. At one time her name had appeared in more end credits than anyone else in television. Oliver had inherited the position in 1996. An outstanding editor of the programme and one of the most gentle and thoughtful men you're ever likely to encounter.

Oliver lived about twenty minutes away. I decided that after my parents and 'best friend' he should be the first person I told. I called to say I needed to come round straight away (I didn't want to tell him why on the phone). He sounded confused but agreed all the same. I left my panicking dad in the flat.

Oliver had taken a bit of a risk in hiring me in the first place – the showreel from Live TV (my previous employer), which I had submitted when applying for the job, showed me in a series of juvenile, tabloidesque stunts, most of which had landed me in trouble. He'd wanted to take on someone a bit cheeky. What he'd got was someone a bit criminal.

He lived on a quiet and immaculately clean, rather prim, nice and well-to-do modern housing estate just outside London. It wasn't the type of place where people got busted in the pages of the *News of the World* (unless perhaps it was a story about suburban swingers).

I remember his wife answering the door, all smiles. Clearly, despite my hints and the urgency of my request, they'd still got no idea of the severity of the situation. 'Richard, come through. Oliver's just listening to *Any Answers* on Radio 4.'

As I entered the living room, a scene of total serenity was laid out before me, starkly contrasting with how I was feeling. Oliver was reclining on his sofa, his dog curled up at his feet, a freshly brewed mug of coffee in hand, listening intently as Jonathan Dimbleby took a tricky question about the legality of British police arresting General Pinochet while he received medical treatment in the United Kingdom.

His wife asked me if I wanted a slice of her home-made lemon drizzle cake.

'Erm, sure. Oliver, I've got some bad news. The *News of the World* is going—'

'Oh don't be ridiculous! Of course they can't arrest Pinochet! Sorry Richard, I love this show.'

'Yeah. The *News of the World* is going to run a story about me taking the drug cocaine and I'm afraid it's a true story. It'll be in the paper tomorrow.'

Oliver didn't seem to be *that* fazed. 'Oh. Right. Well I'm sure we can . . .'

Before he could complete the sentence the enchanting Mrs MacFarlane emerged from the kitchen holding two plates loaded with lemon drizzle cake.[1] Oliver calmly asked me to repeat to her what I'd just told him.

So I told her I'd taken some cocaine and that a story about it was going to be in the newspaper the next day. This is honestly what she said, while proffering me some of that lemon drizzle: 'Oh, this'll just blow over. Everyone smokes that stuff these days.'

Oliver sagely agreed. There was something really touching about the way the two of them were willing the best for me and that they had no idea what cocaine was.

---

[1] Mrs MacFarlane, I am so sorry but I have forgotten your name. I'm sure you'll understand that I had other things on my mind that day, and I just didn't take it in when you introduced yourself. 'Well, I get that, Richard,' I hear you saying, 'yet you seem to have near total recall of what was playing on the radio in our house that day.' Ssssh Mrs MacFarlane (Carol?). And is it too late to thank you for that lemon drizzle cake? Even though I wasn't on my best form, I do recall the cake itself was sublime. You simply *must* send me the recipe.

Suddenly I felt like the parent – I had to shade in some of the understandable gaps in their drugs knowledge. I told Oliver there and then that I didn't see a way out of the situation, other than by me resigning.

I've never been able to eat lemon drizzle cake since without associating it with Oliver's charming wife smoking cocaine (let me stress, she's never done this, it's just the way my mind works).[2]

I don't know how long it took Oliver to get his head around the magnitude of the situation, but he would definitely have figured it out a week later when it was discussed in a language he understood – because a week later I was a topic on *Any Answers* on Radio 4.

I stood there holding an uneaten piece of lemon drizzle cake as he telephoned *his* boss, the controller of Children's BBC, Lorraine Heggessey. Lorraine Heggessey grasped the gravity of the situation instantly.

After the call, Oliver said it didn't look good and that Lorraine was going to call *her* boss, Alan Yentob, who was going to call *his* boss . . . (there's a lot of that at the BBC).

He sent me home and called at 11 p.m. to say that I needed to go to Lorraine's office at midday and that 'it isn't good news'.

I don't remember if I bought a copy of the *News of the World* the next morning. Perhaps not. I'd already seen what they were going to print.

---

[2] On second thoughts, Mrs MacFarlane (Judith?), don't send the recipe.

I do, however, remember the journey to Lorraine's office. It was on the fourteenth floor of 'East Tower', the part of BBC Television Centre (also RIP) then dedicated to children's programming. It's next to the scenery dock and close to 'TC1', which is the biggest studio there. I walked past one of the set builders from *Blue Peter* who was dismantling the scenery from the previous evening's edition of *Noel's House Party*. 'Looking forward to working with you Tuesday, Rich!' he shouted breezily. That didn't help.

I was the first to arrive and so was able to witness the lift open and deposit the three people that had come to see me. Lorraine, Oliver and the head of HR, who was holding my contract in his hand.

Never a good sign.

In the meeting I told Lorraine that I thought I had to go. She asked me to step outside, then invited me back in and told me that she agreed and that, yes, I had to go. There was nothing particularly emotional about this scene. In a crisis things slow down; by now this news story, which others were only just hearing about, already seemed old to me.

As I got up to leave, they had demanded just one more thing of me. This must be the only formality a *Blue Peter* presenter has in common with being in the LAPD – when you leave, they ask you to hand in your badge.

When I walked out of the BBC, I looked back at the front of TV Centre – the one covered in white dots, the one that had filled me with such excitement twenty months previously as I had arrived for my audition – and wondered whether I'd ever be back again. What an idiot I'd been. And what on earth I was going to do now?

You'd think losing my job would be pretty much the end of the story. You'd be wrong. From there on it all got very surreal. And surreal does feel like the best word to describe what unfolded.

The story led the front of *The Sun* for *three days*. The last major headline I recall was '*BLUE PETER* ANNUAL TO BE PULPED.' You know a job's over for good when they're loading your face into an industrial shredder.

For a week, packs of photographers camped outside my house. I went 'into hiding' – tabloid-speak; it means I went to stay with a friend in North London. The *Daily Star* reported I was on 'suicide watch'. The story was absolutely true, bar the fact I wasn't and never had been.

I tuned in Monday morning to my broadcasting hero Chris Evans on the Virgin Radio *Breakfast Show* to hear him discussing me for three hours.

Wednesday evening I was in the Haverstock Arms in Belsize Park (also RIP) when a friend called (not that one) to tell me I was a topic on *Question Time*.

Andrew Carey (who was famous at the time for being 'Andrew the Barman' on *TFI Friday*) flicked on the widescreen telly, normally reserved for football, and everyone in the pub gathered round. They cheered each point that was made in my favour and booed those that weren't. If memory serves (that memory being how to use Google), the exact question from the audience member was: 'Wouldn't it have been more beneficial to put Richard Bacon on *Blue Peter* and show his remorse there, rather than in the newspapers?'

The panel that night was the late film director Michael Winner, the Secretary of State for Wales Ron Davies MP, *The Times*'s Mary Ann Sieghart, Shadow Trade and Industry spokesman John Redwood MP, and Welsh nationalist party Plaid Cymru's Helen Mary Jones.

Everyone was very level-headed on the whole. Mary Ann Sieghart said the furore was 'petty' as I'd 'had a good night out', while John Redwood said my 'agreeing' to be sacked was 'the one decent thing he did in the whole saga'.

I can't remember what Ron Davies said, but he would later become famous for a scandal of his own, when he allegedly had his car stolen by a man he'd met at night on London's Clapham Common.

Unlike Ron, now that the boot is on the other foot, I will not idly ponder the rights and wrongs of his scandal in a public forum. (I'm not, I'm just enjoying having the moral high ground for once in this chapter).

While it's difficult to convey what being at the centre of a media storm is like, if you are intrigued by how the media operates, which I was and am, then it was an absolutely fascinating week. Although that fascination is more than offset by the uncertainty, the fear of what's next, what's around the corner – one moment you'll hear a reporter has turned up on the doorstep of some old school friend you haven't been in touch with for years, another that photographers are hiding in the bushes outside your mum and dad's house.

Mum and Dad were also interviewed on the telly. Until recently I'd thought their utter dismay at what had happened had been briefly alleviated by the painkilling properties of being asked to appear on ITV's *News at Ten*. Looking like hostages in a terrorist video (if that terrorist video had been filmed in a rather comfortable looking, aspirational middle-class house in Mansfield), they had the rare honour of appearing as the third bong in the opening titles: a headline read by Trevor McDonald's voice booming ('the sacked *Blue Peter* presenter's parents speak out . . .') over footage of them walking solemnly and inexplicably past the birdbath in their garden.

They have made a few radio and TV appearances in their time. They love it. And knowing them as I do, I believed that they had enjoyed this – the excitement of being on *News at Ten* with old Trev (a moment of pure showbiz in an otherwise terrible maelstrom). In an email exchange with my mum ahead of writing this story, she corrected that assumption:

> It's a bit unfair to suggest we were loving the limelight. Dad didn't want to do it. I persuaded him to do it because we were hounded and hounded, and I thought maybe the pressure would shift if we spoke. Also, I wanted to say what I did – that you had made a

mistake – but I still loved you. Although me saying I still loved you was scorned on by a columnist in one of the broadsheets. I think you have to understand that we were in a whirl – not for a minute did appearing on *News at Ten*, re: your own son, seem 'fun'. I woke up at every morning at 4 a.m. with awful stomach pains and was convinced the shock of the whole episode had given me cancer! I worried about Dad, and had to stay strong for him.

Reading that back makes me feel guilty even now. It certainly doesn't sound like fun.

I was the subject of the story. They were not. And yet, and I imagine this is true for anyone who's been the subject of a scandal with a mum and dad who are still around, it is always worse for them.

Which brings me to the worst aspect of this saga.

My dad is not a man who displays emotion easily, or regularly. Nor do I, especially. He's a quite brilliant man – a solicitor from a working-class background who's built a flawless reputation, clever, incorruptible, thoughtful, caring and kind (my carefree approach to life is a product of the perfect upbringing he and Mum provided), but none of us has ever seen him get emotional or cry. We're not a family who hug each other or talk about our deepest feelings.

On the Monday morning, with the story still leading all the tabloids, and even some broadsheets, my dad was getting ready to go to work down at Mansfield's

Magistrate's court, with people who know him well when my mum overheard him weeping in the shower. She told me that in thirty-five years of knowing him, it was the first time she had *ever* heard him cry. Writing this down, it's only the second time I've let myself think about it – and it still makes me feel ashamed.

A day later, the moment the credits on *Newsround* came to an end, Lorainne Heggessey appeared on BBC1, sitting in her office, making what appeared to be an address to the nation. Sounding not unlike the Queen she quietly said, 'I believe that Richard has not only let himself and the team on *Blue Peter* down, but he's also let all of you down badly.'

The programme cut from Lorraine's office back to Kirsten O'Brien in the CBBC broom cupboard, who announced that *Blue Peter* that day was featuring Stuart Miles' 'visit Uganda'. I might have let down the children of Great Britain, but even I would have drawn the line at sending an openly gay man to Uganda.

The *News of the World* wanted a follow-up to the story which they'd been running throughout the week. But with me out of the picture and *Blue Peter* populated by junior clergy, they doorstepped the man behind the CBBC puppet Otis the Aardvark the following Saturday to ask him if *he'd* ever taken any cocaine. He hadn't. Although, if he had wanted to, Otis the Aardvark had the perfect, naturally occurring equipment for the job.

Back on *Blue Peter*, they briefly mentioned that they

were going to miss me, and a few weeks later unveiled my replacement: Simon Thomas, the son of a vicar. Added to Katy Hill, this meant that fifty per cent of *Blue Peter*'s presenters were now offspring of the clergy. They weren't taking *any* chances.

I watched the show that went out that week – my first show as a former *Blue Peter* presenter. Following a segment about futuristic cars they cut back to the studio. 'As you probably know,' said Katy Hill, dressed in a red jumpsuit, '*Blue Peter* has been in the news a lot recently. Firstly, last week, we were celebrating our fortieth birthday' (the show, not Katy).

They then showed off a special Bafta that had been awarded to the show for its 'Outstanding Services to Children's Television' over the past forty years – an award that was created specifically for *Blue Peter* and which will never be won by any other show.

Then the mood changed. Stuart Miles turned to a different camera and said in grave tones: 'But there is also some sad news. You'll no doubt have heard that Richard is no longer on the programme.'

'Yes', Katy chimed in. 'He agrees he had to leave, and like you we are really going to miss him.'

It was handled with all the professionalism you'd expect from *Blue Peter* but, regrettably, it did leave a lot of children asking awkward questions such as, 'Mummy, what's a Bafta? Why are there special Baftas just for kids' shows?'. And, most heartbreaking of all: 'Daddy, isn't having a dedicated children's Bafta demeaning to the value of a genuine one?'[3]

In the days and weeks afterwards, I received hundreds of letters from kids. Lots of them very touching. A couple of years ago the actress Sienna Miller told me that she wrote to the BBC to protest the decision to fire me.

The kids who wrote those letters would now be in their mid-twenties. I didn't reply to them individually at the time, because I knew, one day, I'd have my own book in which I could thank them all in one convenient lot. So here goes. Thanks, pals.[4] (If some newspaper editorials from the time were correct, my 'role model' status means that you are all now drug addicts so sadly, long before you even reached the 'Thanks, pals' bit you'd probably pawned the book).

The following weekend was my mum's fiftieth birthday and she'd hired out the dining room of a Derbyshire hotel to celebrate. None of our family or friends thought I would make it, but I surprised her by arriving halfway through with a bouquet of flowers. As I entered to give Mum a hug and the flowers, the whole room stood up and applauded. It was a lump-in-the-throat moment, like a scene from *Dead Poets Society* with an added drugs-shame bit.

Even now, fourteen years later, every couple of weeks some dullard will make an entry-level humorous quip from the window of a van. 'Oi Bacon, got any beak?' (Sometimes they say it to make their mates laugh and sometimes they clearly mean it, which is worse because

---

[3] Don't get me started on Scottish Baftas.

[4] If you didn't write me a letter, please cross out the phrase 'Thanks, pals.'

it suggests they think I'm some sort of part-time dealer.) Not one of these boorish people has had the courtesy to also mention the special Bafta that I co-won that weekend. 'Oi Bacon, fancy a special Bafta?' Never heard that one. Not once.

So that's it. And it's a story I hope I never have to tell again.

But I know, deep in my heart of hearts, that it's the one thing about me that will always be there. When I die and a newspaper writes an obituary about me (making a bit of a grand assumption there), irrespective of what I go on to do – bring peace to the Middle East, cure cancer, invent the teleporter – the summary at the top of the piece will say:

RICHARD BACON
The only presenter ever to be sacked from Blue Peter. *(Oh, and he invented the teleporter).*

Jesus, I'm glad that's out of the way.

Now – enjoy the rest of the book.

Chapter 2

TELL 'IM HE'S A MURDERER

One day, somebody at the *Daily Mirror*, with a big sack of cash they were dying to invest badly, decided to set up a network cable TV channel.

It was called Live TV (the 'i' in the logo was replaced with an exclamation mark, but I never liked the look of it and believe it is beneath the dignity of this book to write it as such. You are free to go through this chapter with a pen and some Tippex and amend Live TV as you see fit).

They were openly looking for young, untrained, starry-eyed, cheap staff to front and make their programmes.

That's where BBC Radio Nottingham's junior reporter Richard Bacon came in.

The office was on the twenty-fourth floor of Canary Wharf Tower – quite an exciting place to work, as a twenty year old.

My job interview was conducted by Nick Ferrari. London readers will be familiar with his avuncular style of presenting on the LBC *Breakfast Show*. His wry little bons mots include calling for income tax for human rights lawyers to be doubled. He was and is an intimidating presence, in a way that tabloid hacks of that generation really were, and still are.

He's turned himself into a very effective and successful radio broadcaster, but if you've heard him you'll understand why a job interview with him is quite frightening.

He asked me what sort of reporting I had been responsible for at BBC Radio Nottingham.

I told him that I had been sent to cover the story of a local English teacher that very week, whose school football team had topped some sort of national league.

And that to make the story more interesting, I had made up a key detail by claiming that the teacher shouted Shakespeare puns at his players to inspire them.

'Once more unto the goal, dear players. Two nil or not two nil. A plague on both your defenders.' That sort of rubbish.

I had even talked the teacher into playing along with my deception.

Nick thought this was entirely consistent with the values of Live TV (in that it was nonsense and not particularly witty).

Sitting on Nick's office table was a copy of that day's *Sun* where, by fortuitous coincidence, my fabrication had been picked up, in no way fact-checked, and run across page eight. They had even illustrated the story by sticking the Bard's head onto the body of a football player to further clarify what was already an extremely easy-to-grasp concept.

Nick bloody loved it. It is worth pausing to reflect that this was back in the glory days when the BBC, a cable TV channel and the country's biggest tabloid paper could join hands and celebrate a lie as one.

These days you can't lie to the listeners. Is the world really a better place because of that? I don't think you need me to answer that question. (Just in case you couldn't see what I was hinting at, the answer's no. You used to be able to say any old shit.)

Nick's ultimate boss was the former editor of *The Sun*, Kelvin MacKenzie. I liked working for him. We were not going to share many views, but he's blunt, he's witty and he's totally uncompromising. And out of the combustible, volatile atmosphere over which he and Nick presided emerged some occasionally very good ideas. And loads of absolutely wretched ones.

If you have any interest in tabloid newspapers at all and haven't yet read *Stick It Up Your Punter!*, then you're in for a treat.

This is a quote from Kelvin taken from that book on the subject of how he perceived his readers at *The Sun* during his time there in the 1980s:

He's the bloke you see in the pub, a right old fascist, wants to send the wogs back, buys his poxy council house, he's afraid of the unions, afraid of the Russians, hates the queers and the weirdos and drug dealers.[5]

But what Live TV lacked in money and experience, it more than made up for in poor programming.

Inspired by the success of *Neighbours*, Live TV commissioned a daily soap opera. It is officially the lowest ever budgeted British soap. It was called *Canary Wharf*. You probably can't remember how *Canary Wharf* concluded. *Canary Wharf* concluded with Canary Wharf Tower being taken into space. It's all there on YouTube.

There was no money for a set so, every now and again, on the end of the bank of desks at which I was writing the news bulletin a couple of 'actors' would start simulating sex for a scene in a forthcoming episode.

During the BSE crisis in 1996 – if you can't remember, it was not unlike that horsemeat scandal but mercifully pre-Twitter, so there weren't seven thousand lazy jokes by amateur stand-ups about it – when it was revealed that some British beef was carrying Creutzfeldt–Jakob disease, the *Daily Mirror* ran a front claiming that McDonald's was almost alone in continuing to sell British beef. Everyone else at the time had cleared their shelves of the stuff. Kelvin marched up to me in the newsroom, pointed

---

[5] Peter Chippindale and Chris Horrie, *Stick It Up Your Punter: The Rise and Fall of The Sun* (London: Faber, 2013).

out of the twenty-fourth-floor window of Canary Wharf Tower (then not in space) to the McDonald's on the Isle of Dogs.

'Go down there,' he bellowed, 'ask for the manager, and when he comes out you tell 'im he's a MURDERER. Tell 'im that by continuing to sell British beef he is a murderer! Got it?'

I did as I was commanded, and was thrown out and banned from the McDonald's on the Isle of Dogs. As a twenty-year-old living, at that time, on the Isle of Dogs, that ban cut me off from one of my main sources of food (actually the fast turnover of staff at those places means bans don't really work – if you've been banned, go back).

If you know anything about Live TV you'll know that it's mascot was the 'News Bunny', which was a man in a rabbit suit who would stand behind the newsreader and put his thumbs up if the story he was talking about was a nice one and down when it wasn't.

As a publicity stunt, the News Bunny was made to stand in the Staffordshire East by-election. But candidates for political office have to stand under their real names and, when the results came in, Kelvin wanted the returning officer to say 'Mr News Bunny', the thinking being that those words would then be broadcast on real, much-watched TV news programmes covering the results. The strategy seemed to be that if any viewer heard 'Mr News Bunny' mentioned by a returning officer while watching (for example) Newsnight, they would immediately abandon terrestrial television for Live TV's simplistic and adolescent output. So Ashley Hames, the man inside the rabbit suit, changed his name by deed poll to News Bunny. And for some bureaucratic reason he couldn't change it back for a year (even his credit cards read 'Mr. N. Bunny').

I sat with Kelvin in the control room and watched a live feed of News Bunny (né Ashley) out campaigning. He was handing out leaflets in the middle of the road, blocking the traffic, telling people they could have 'free carrots' as the police kept telling him to move. He just ignored them, which was really making Kelvin laugh – I laughed too, as the Dear Leader was laughing, and laughing along with him was obligatory, although it *was* also funny.

After a couple of minutes the police arrested him for obstruction.

Kelvin collapsed in hysterics.

You know when the police put someone they've arrested into the back of the squad car and they tend to place a hand on the back of the accused's head to guide them into the back seat? Well, we watched as a copper, who for some reason didn't ask Ashley to remove his rabbit head, did exactly that to the News Bunny, carefully folding down his ears.

This might say something about my nature, but seeing the boss of a company giggle uncontrollably as he watched one of his own employees being arrested as a stunt went wrong (or right?) made me realise that for its litany of faults, I rather admired the spirit of Live TV.

Anyway, obstruction was the least of News Bunny's crimes. Far more seriously, he got me banned from both Houses of Parliament.

I'd turned up to cover the State Opening with him. All the lords were dripping with ermine and mink, so News Bunny didn't seem entirely out of place, but after the event Black Rod (which isn't *his* real name either and sounds no less silly) sent me a now-framed letter telling me I'd trivialised the event and so was banned from Parliament. It appears there's one rule for the aristocracy and quite another for employees of the 'piss-poor L!ve TV' (*Private Eye*).

In 2012 I made a BBC documentary about Internet trolling, and a couple of friends told me they were pleased to see me making my first documentary. It shocked me that these so-called 'friends' were that unfamiliar with my œuvre. This was *not* my *first* documentary. I made my first in 1996. It was called *Behind the Scenes of Topless Darts on Ice*.

It was the heart-warming story of two breasts that dreamed of being exposed on an ice rink while their owner attempted to play darts. If, like my friends, you never saw *Topless Darts On Ice*, you'll be pleased to know that the dream of these two breasts came true in the end. I don't know where they are today, but I hope they are happy.

Despite being a TV station, it was quite surprising what scant attention people paid to what was broadcast and when. Much of the content was pre-recorded but made to look live (another lie that television isn't allowed to get away with anymore). I sat in the office watching the output – something staff very, very rarely did – and noticed we were transmitting a 'live' programme fronted by Larry Grayson. A good signing for Live TV: Larry 'shut that door' Grayson, who made his name triumphantly taking over from Bruce Forsyth on *The Generation Game*. Quite the coup. And even more of a coup when you consider that the man fronting that 'live' show, Larry 'shut that door' Grayson, had died the previous weekend. A door had indeed been shut. By God. And a programme had been put out. By an idiot.

By the time I left for my next job over at *Blue Peter*, people were being sacked left, right and centre, and no one really knew what was going on. What was apparent to everyone was that Live TV wasn't working. At one point it was losing £7 million a year and the shows which were, in the main, bad to begin with were getting worse.

In one final, last-gasp attempt of misplaced and daring ambition, Live TV bid for the rights to the Premiership. That's right, THE Premiership. In case you didn't know, they failed to secure them. They could barely hang on to *Topless Darts on Ice*. After four years, Live TV was closed down.

If Live TV had been given a funeral, it would have been buried in a pauper's grave. The handful of mourners would have included a man in a rabbit suit, a dwarf broadcaster with a trampoline under his arm, not bouncing on it as a mark of respect, a Norwegian weather girl in a veil with her boobs out and a fifty-five-year-old unemployed pervert from Scarborough – the channel's only remaining viewer.

The gravestone would not have had anything like the budget it needed. And the slogan would have read 'Here lies L!ve TV. It's in a better place now – i.e. not on the television.'

Chapter 3

WOULD YOU LIKE CRIES WITH THAT?

In *A la recherche du temps perdu*, Marcel Proust is spirited back to his childhood memories of consuming a madeleine cake.

> No sooner had the warm liquid mixed with the crumbs touched my palate than a shudder ran through me and I stopped, intent upon the extraordinary thing that was happening to me . . . Suddenly the memory revealed itself. The taste was that of the little piece of madeleine which . . . my aunt Léonie used to give me . . . The sight of the little madeleine had recalled nothing to my mind before I tasted it.[6]

---

[6] Marcel Proust, *In Search of Lost Time*, trans. C. K. Scott Moncrieff, Terence Kilmartin and Andreas Mayor, revsd D. J. Enright (London: Chatto & Windus; New York: The Modern Library, 1992).

I once sat on an industrial-size catering pack of pre-sliced McDonald's gherkins in the stock room of a Mansfield branch, bawling my eyes out because my heart had been broken for the first time.

For Proust, that madeleine cake contained the essence of the past. For me, the essence of the past is contained in a sliver of a McDonald's gherkin.

No sooner has the brine-preserved slice from a McDonald's hamburger – and/or cheeseburger (I sometimes have both), or one of the *two* that come in a quarter-pounder – touched my palate than a shudder runs through me and the memory reveals itself . . . the memory of Rachel.

Rachel made Sienna Miller look like Arthur Miller. Mulligan, Carey look like former Archbishop of Canterbury George Carey (I had to reverse her name to make that work). She made the Dani Behr of the early-1990s look like the Dani Behr of the mid-2000s. I really fancied Rachel. And Rachel really fancied me.

And why wouldn't she? I was quite a catch. I had a minimum-wage job working Friday and Saturday nights in one of the more volatile branches of that fast-food empire.

So volatile that every Friday and Saturday night the police would park a riot van outside the front door in anticipation of the trouble that would invariably kick off inside.

So volatile that staff would frequently have to miss their shifts because they were testifying in court as witnesses to some horrible assault.

So volatile that I'd sometimes take one customer's order as they rammed another's head into the counter beneath my till.

But that customer in the headlock and I came to have *something in common* – we would both forever associate McDonald's of Mansfield with pain.

Rachel broke my heart inside that McDonald's and in doing so ruined for me a job that I loved. And I mean really loved.

In the first few days of my eighteen-month stint, I was tipped for big things. The 'training manager' (one up from five stars, you get a white badge, the McDonald's equivalent of the US military's three-star general) told me that I was so enthusiastic, so good that I would earn all five stars (till, cleaning, front of house, kitchen, back room) within six months. *Just* six months. I realise you don't know how long it normally takes for someone to earn five stars and so that doesn't mean much to you. Well, let me tell you, it's good. Bloody good. But here's the tragedy. After a year and a half, I had been awarded just the ONE STAR (till).

Such wasted promise. Just thrown away. I was the Mansfield McDonald's equivalent of Gazza.

And, like Gazza, I started *brilliantly*. On day one I was completely awed by how McDonald's worked.

Regular meat (that's the meat that goes into hamburgers, cheeseburgers and Big Macs) goes from frozen to fully cooked in 42–44 seconds.

Just stop and think about that for a minute (which is a third longer than the time it takes to cook McDonald's cheeseburgers). Frozen to fully cooked in forty-two to forty-four seconds.

And quarter-pounder meat?

A quarter of a pound of frozen meat is ready for your digestive system in sixty-four seconds.

Even now, at thirty-six, double the age I was then, I recount that fact to people with the exact same sense of wonder and reverence I felt then.

My enthusiasm had set me fair for a flourishing career within McDonald's. I remember a chap, it might have been that 'training manager', who'd completed his A-levels and had his heart set on taking a degree in Law.

But he'd taken a year out from his education to save up some cash from a job at Mansfield McDonald's. A good place to see law in action up close. But he loved Mansfield McDonald's *so much* that he ditched that law degree and stayed on. And the last time I checked he was still there.

Isn't that a lovely story?

And that could have been me.

But then, something changed.

In *Death of a Salesman* by the aforementioned Arthur Miller, the lead character Willy Loman's son Biff is doing well at college and on course for great things until something sends him off course. (He catches his dad with a woman: if you've not seen it yet, and are worried I've ruined it, you've only got yourself to blame. It's been out since 1949.)

Like Biff Loman, a traumatic experience ruined everything for me.

Rachel. Ruined. Everything.

It was a quiet Friday evening in Mansfield town centre (by 'quiet' I mean there had only been two affrays and three common assaults). Dutiful as ever, I was standing at my station, for this shift at the till, serving customers and serving them effortlessly, when Rachel approached the counter.

We'd been together for about a year at this point.

Before she even spoke I began tapping in her favourite order (cheeseburger and regular fries with a sweet-and-sour sauce). I'd always do a clever sleight of hand with the till so my darling wouldn't have to pay. The major perk of working for McDonald's is giving food away to your mates. Some people call this theft. Not me.

She looked worried, but I just presumed that was the natural human response to being in the Mansfield branch of McDonald's on a Friday night.

She'd have known that the tally of affrays and common assaults was preternaturally low that night. It would unsettle anyone. But I was wrong. It wasn't that.

'Richard,' she whispered solemnly, 'there's something I need to say.'

'Don't worry, babes!' (Back in 1994, 'babes' was totally acceptable, Operation Yewtree.) 'I've already rung it up!'

'No, Richard . . .'

Before she got any more words out I had turned around and begun assembling her order.

Cheeseburger first, carefully making sure it hadn't been left standing for more than twenty minutes, before placing it in a small brown McDonald's bag. Over to the fries 'station' next. There were few things more frustrating in that job than getting to the fry station to discover that not only were there none left, but that the last person to use it hadn't put any more in the fryer. Asa, you were particularly poor at that. No such problem this time. I carefully added the fries, retrieved a sweet-and-sour from beneath my counter, folded the top of the bag over twice to form a shallow lip in the house style and handed it to Rachel with a broad, self-satisfied smile on my face. The food might have been stolen, but I *never* compromised my high standards of service.

She took the bag in her left hand and told me our relationship was over. I can't remember the exact words but it was pretty brutal. If you've ever had your heart broken, you might know that sensation of feeling as though you have been winded.

If the police are reading this let me make something clear: Rachel was in receipt of, and later consumed, stolen goods to the value of whatever a cheeseburger, regular fries and a sweet-and-sour sauce was in 1994. She had also accepted stolen food on a number of previous occasions. I don't know if the statute of limitations means you can't act, but it would certainly be worth you, at the very least, liaising with the CPS.

Being dumped is traumatic anyway – and worse in public. But nothing is quite as humiliating as being dumped in public, while you're wearing a red-and-white-striped McDonald's shirt, a little red hat that doesn't fit you properly, a dog-eared badge with your first name printed on it above the words 'Can I Help You Please?' and stinking of grease.

I raced to the stockroom where I sat, crying my eyes out, on a box of Marcel Proust's gherkins (you know what I mean).

But it wasn't just my relationship with Rachel that soured that day. It was my relationship with McDonald's.

As Biff Loman would understand, from that day on, I became one of the worst and laziest employees that McDonald's UK has ever had the misfortune to hire (and just think of the ground that statement covers).

A man whose dedication to the service of giving drunk people burgers had been unwavering – well, that man just gave up.

That idealistic young fellow, so fired up in the heady excitement of those first couple of weeks on the job, spent the next sixty-four doing almost nothing.

The projected five stars in six months was, as you already know, but a pipe dream.

So lackadaisical and inattentive was I that one evening a pisshead staggered in and asked for a Filet-O-Fish without cheese . . . But before I explain what happened I should tell you that this is *every* McDonald's staff member's nightmare scenario.

The Filet-O-Fish takes longer than any other burger to cook. It means a minimum of eight minutes. (If you're one of the fools who orders it without cheese, know this: there's only half a slice of processed cheese on there anyway. Order the pre-prepared one and *peel the cheese off*, otherwise we have to make it from scratch.)

So I took his order and he paid. With thoughts of resentment towards McDonald's and the absence of sex with Rachel swirling around my head, I went on my one-hour break. I came back, pottered around for ten minutes and noticed Pisshead was still sitting there.

His cheeseless Filet-O-Fish had long since disappeared from the kitchen.

So I had to reorder it, adding a further eight minutes to the total. He'd now been waiting one hour and sixteen minutes. And this tells you everything you need to know about the customers who came into McDonald's of Mansfield on a Friday and Saturday night: I fronted it out, didn't apologise, casually handed him his Filet-O-Fish, and all he said was 'Thanks.'

As I watched that man drunkenly weave his way past a man being tossed into the back of the police riot van stationed at the front door, I knew it was time to quit.

I should have quit *the day* I found myself crying on an industrial-size pack of pre-sliced gherkins.

Because that was the day that everything changed, and it is why it's impossible for me to crunch through the gherkin in a McDonald's hamburger without feeling pain in my heart.

A pain that has nothing to do with the high levels of saturated fat packed inside every delicious, juicy meat patty.

And what happened to Rachel? The answer is, I don't know.

But wherever she is now and whatever she's doing, I sincerely hope one thing: that some day she decides to look me up, put pen to paper, and apologise for her disgraceful behaviour.[7]

---

[7] I will not accept her apology.

Chapter 4

DEAD GRANDMAS SAY THE FUNNIEST THINGS

I should state for the record that, until I met 'Britain's best-loved psychic'[8], I did not believe that living people could communicate with the dead.

I used to be one of those close-minded people who don't believe in the paranormal. Mediums, crystal balls, runes, tarot cards, table wobbling, wearing a headscarf – I thought it was all very silly. And I admit, my scepticism was part of the reason I was looking forward to encountering someone who claimed to have psychic abilities.

I was not a believer. And then, I met Sally Morgan.

Sally says she can speak to your dead relatives. No, sorry, she doesn't 'say' she can speak to your dead

---

[8] That is how I have seen Sally billed. I would have thought it would be better to be billed as 'Britain's most accurate psychic', or 'Britain's most stringently tested', or 'Britain's only genuine'. If I'm going to communicate with my dead grandma, the loveable-ness of a medium isn't much more than a fringe issue. It'd be like being 'Britain's most punctual chef': it's not entirely irrelevant, but it's not the number one quality I look for in a chef.

relatives. As I now know, she can and *does* speak to your dead relatives.

A few years ago, I agreed to take part in a television show of hers on ITV2. She came along to Capital Radio, producers and crew for the programme in tow and gave me a reading on the terrace atop Capital's seven-storey building. (I presume this venue was chosen because it's closer to heaven, and she'd therefore hear the dead a little bit better.)

The reading lasted about twenty minutes and I was immediately struck by the accuracy of her hit rate. The number of correct statements she came up with was much higher than you would expect if someone was, say, just guessing wildly. There was simply enough in there that was correct, about my work, my new relationship and a recent house move that she could only have known about if she:

(a) was actually in contact with the shadowy world of the departed and was conversing with the dead who walk, ever vigilant, amongst the oblivious living, or

(b) had had a brief chat with my new girlfriend (and wife-to-be) Rebecca in reception before coming up to see me.

Although it could have been a combination of both because now, Sally had, it later turned out, had a bit of a chat with my new girlfriend (and wife-to-be) Rebecca in reception before coming to see me. Is that reason enough to dismiss her? No, dear reader. No it is not. I won't let that trifling coincidence sway me.

That's because I've let this sway me. In 2012, Sally announced that she going to sue the *Daily Mail* over an article where the magician Paul Zenon said he was 'sceptical' of Sally's powers, and stated that 'if heaven forbid, performers like Ms Morgan aren't actually talking to the dead . . . then I think the public has a right to know.' Through solicitors Atkins Thomson, Sally demanded damages of £150,000.

So let me be absolutely clear in case Sally or a member of her legal team from Atkins Thomson are reading this book: the information she gave me about my work, my new relationship and a recent house move can *only* have come from the dead (although admittedly, as Rebecca remembers very clearly, a couple of the smaller, trivial things had come from Sally's conversation with her, but only a couple).

Very specifically, as Sally explained, that information came directly from my mum's mum, whose name was (and presumably still is?) Jennie.

She does not use any of the tricks or techniques outlined at length by Paul Zenon in that *Daily Mail* article (it's still online). I can state with one hundred per cent certainty that she spoke to my dead grandma, who I rather casually used to refer to as Jennie, and everything Sally said about me and my life came from Jennie, who was speaking to me through the medium of a medium.

Sure, there was some absolute rubbish that Sally came out with, things she said about me that were miles out. Thankfully, the TV viewers never actually *saw* Sally get much wrong – because mostly what I disputed was omitted from the finished TV broadcast. And I entirely understand why this was so.

Sally was receiving all this information – both wrong and right – directly from my grandmother's spirit. So it would be silly to be annoyed with Sally for putting this confusing information out there – as the saying goes, 'Don't shoot the messenger!' (although if you did, Sally would then be able to communicate with them.) The blame for these nonsensical utterances lies entirely at Jennie's feet, if you still have feet when you're a ghost. I don't know if you still need feet in the afterlife, because I think you get wings (to be honest, this is really something you'd need to ask Sally about).

Regardless of it being entirely my grandmother's fault, I know, dead or alive, Jennie would not have wanted to look stupid on television, and so, to spare her blushes, the production company kindly took the decision to cut any mistakes that she conveyed through Sally. Thus, in the final edit, it appeared as though Sally had only passed on information that was (mostly) correct. And on behalf of my late grandma, I'd like to thank the production team for that act of kindness.

And there's a lesson for all dead people here. If you're talking to Sally, or any other medium for that matter (Derek Acorah, Colin Fry, the guy I saw in Edinburgh who was all over the shop), you *must* speak more clearly. You simply must.

How can mediums be expected to get the name of

someone's childhood dog right if you're mumbling? And if it takes them more than two or three goes, it just ends up with non-psychic people thinking the whole 'speaking-to-the-dead' thing is just a load of garbage.

And that's not fair on Britain's hard-working, con-scientious, genuine mediums.

I don't know if the dead go senile, but that *would* explain why many of the dead who speak through Sally and her friends often get their own names wrong, misremember what their loved ones are called, and aren't very exact regarding dates, places, or manners of death. If you're in heaven, try not to let the ones who've gone a bit infirm chat with the psychic – it makes everyone look bad.

And there's another thing I've had just about enough of from you dead people. Not only do you communicate hit-and-miss stuff about our relatives through Sally and her colleagues, you also like to spend a lot of time predicting the future. There's *nothing* the dead like to do more when they've got the mouthpiece of a medium than take a 50/50 hit-it-and-hope punt on the sex of a family baby on the way. I didn't think dying granted you the power to see into the future but, clearly, I don't know much about this sort of thing, not being a medium myself. Or dead. But I think you should stop guessing at baby gender, as more often than not you're wrong – even though the odds are 50/50.

And while we're on the subject, there's something else I'd like to pick you spirit beings up on. After years of silence, you need to think more carefully about the sort of information you're going to pass on.

One of the sole, very specific things my grandmother told Sally was the amount of money I'd just spent on a house. Sally said the information she'd received was something to do with a house: 'Richard, I'm seeing a one . . . (a pause on Sally's part, just in case my dead grandmother had finished speaking and I was about to jump in and say, 'Yes, it's Number one!' . . . 'and a four.'

I told Sally that I'd put in a sealed bid of £1.4 million for a house *that very morning*. (She had not got that from Rebecca, I checked, I don't believe there was any cheating going on. So, tip of the hat this was, as we all on the radio show agree, a pretty impressive moment even if Sally hadn't specifically said she was guessing the cost of the house. Sorry, not 'guessing', 'communicating with the dead to find out'.)

But Jennie, it would have made all our lives easier and shot any sceptic's fox if you'd related *exactly* what you'd seen, given that, as Sally explained, you had been at my side *every single* moment since your death ten years ago. And as you'd seen the actual transaction going down, you could have been really specific without blurting out the cost.

For example, you should have said to Sally, 'Tell Richard I'm really excited for him after he put in his sealed bid this morning for a house in Belsize Park with the estate agents Benham and Reeves. I was glad to see it was accepted on the second bid.'

Instead, the alienating sum of money I'd spent on my house was broadcast to the viewers of ITV2 just so you could prove you were there. I would rather, if I'm honest with you Jennie, that it had not come out.[9]

Three years after that rooftop experience, Sally was a guest on my BBC Radio 5 Live programme – and, much to my surprise, grandmother Jennie got back in touch. We'd not spoken for three years (I was still annoyed she had gone and told ITV2's viewers the cost of my house), but I decided to let bygones be bygones. After all, we're talking about family here.

Sally began talking a lot about Jennie's (remember, dead), husband Jack (also dead) and handily my mum Christine (not dead.) So, during the travel bulletin, I called my mum and put her on air with Sally.

Sally told my mum that Jennie (her mum) had given birth to a son who died young. This was quite the bombshell. My mum has an older sister, but now Sally was telling my mum she had a brother she never knew about.

When Mum told Sally she was certain that wasn't the

---

[9] During the recording on the roof of Capital Radio, the moment I said, 'Well, I have just put in a bid of £1.4 million,' I realised that this was an entirely alienating sum to broadcast on television. So I leaned to my left, peered round the camera, made eye contact with the producer (something which I thought signalled an off-air conversation) and said, 'Don't put that in, it'll make me look like a twat.' When I watched the show being broadcast, in the bit where they tease part two at the end of part one, the voiceover said: 'Coming up – Sally finds out something sensitive about DJ Richard Bacon.' And it cut to me saying, 'Well, I have just put in a bid of £1.4 million. (PAUSE.) Don't put that in, it'll make me look like a twat.' I can only presume the producer had the reverse gift to Sally Morgan, in that he was unable to hear clearly worded requests from the living.

case, Jennie once again started to muddy the waters by telling Sally that this dead boy *could* be from my mum's side of the family, but *might* be from my dad's side of the family. With my mum still not biting, Jennie added through Sally that *thinking about it*, the dead boy might even have been a generation further back.

It is disappointing that Jennie had trouble remembering the specific details of this story, given that it was either her child or it wasn't.

Mum valiantly tried to help her out. 'Maybe you mean my *grandmother* – she couldn't carry boys. She'd carried two boys, but neither of them made it to full term and they died before they were born. But I can't think of any living boy or child that was lost in our family.'

Ignoring Mum's helpful lifeline, Sally went for something else entirely. 'What about August the third, is August third connected to the grandma?'

'No.'

Sally had a very sage response to my mum not recognising any of these suggestions: 'Sometimes you have to think about it. We have just chucked this straight at you, Christine.'

Suddenly, Jennie must have hung up, because now Sally was talking directly to my mum's father, or at least she had a real 'sense' of him. I'm not sure what the distinction is but we quickly found out through Sally that he was a very 'strong character'. It's hard to imagine a better way of describing him. Sorry, I don't mean 'imagine', I mean 'it's hard to convey a better sense of what he was actually like if you found yourself talking to him.'

I asked Sally to tell me something about my granddad. 'Rather than just tell us you have a sense of him, tell me, what did my granddad do for a living? How did he die?' It was, Sally told us (and this can only have come via my grandfather Jack himself) something to do with 'the side of his head'. Which was a revelation to Mum and me, because he appeared to have died of alcoholism. Bloody Jack! Even death couldn't stop him joking around! (Something he didn't really do while he was alive.)

In fact, nearly everything Sally heard from Jennie and Jack turned out to be, at best, completely new. She told my mum she'd had a brother she'd never known about, although it might have been an uncle. This was a revelation so shocking that absolutely no one in the family had any idea about it, or proof of it, or thought it had ever happened.

But Sally told us that one day in the future, we'd get proof. That day still hasn't come, but she told us when that day came, we'd see that she was right. And until then, we should probably believe her. Now a cynic might argue that the line of logic that MANY OF A PSYCHIC'S PREDICTIONS will one day turn out to be true given an unspecified amount of time, is an easy get out. But I, dear reader, am not a cynic[10].

---

[10] This is why I already know that my son is going to have a sex change. Sally told me that my first child would be 'a daughter'. She just didn't say when.

And with that in mind, I'm now going to address my grandmother Jennie directly.

Jennie, rather than blurt out a piece of sensitive information to a stranger that was then repeated on ITV2, or introduce unverifiable family stories that you'd kept to yourself throughout your life but suddenly, and for no apparent reason, wanted to reveal when you were dead, why not say something useful, or loving, or exciting?

I don't need to be told how much money I've offered for my own house. I know. But I would like to know what it's like to be dead. Come on? Do you sleep? Are there restaurants? Is there a government? A president of dead people? There's a good pool of deceased world leaders to choose from. What skills down here are useful up there? You can tell me definitively if there's a heaven and hell. Jennie, you could have told me that instead of mentioning something about 'August 3$^{rd'}$* and half-baked allegations about you perhaps giving birth.*

But you didn't.

Instead you decided up on that roof of Capital Radio to piss about telling me (much of which, thankfully, wasn't broadcast to spare your embarrassment) that I was going to propose to my girlfriend by a loch (I didn't), that I go running 'a bit too often' and that I 'go abroad a lot'. That's no use to me, Jennie. No fucking use at all.

Look Jennie, I was an excellent grandson. I used to visit you twice a week at your house. I used to pick up your pension. I mowed your lawn and in your latter years I was the most frequent visitor to that residential care home you were in. You're dead. You must have something canny or insightful to say about it. You know what it's like to be alive. I don't know what it's like to be dead. So next time we speak, tell me something interesting, that's all I ask.

At least I know Jennie will get to read this plea. No, not because this book will be big in heaven, but because, as I type these words, Jennie is reading them over my shoulder.

Don't panic, it's not like in *Psycho*; I haven't kept her body. Sally reminded me more than once that Jennie's been at my side in spirit ever since her mortal body left this earth.

So Jennie, I know you are with me now and can see what I'm writing – although I am writing this bit in the new private members' club Little House in London's Mayfair, and you could easily be distracted by Nick Hewer who's sitting by the fire. (Oh, Jennie, if that is what you're doing, grow up. Nick Hewer has made it abundantly clear time and again that he will not date the dead.) But assuming you are reading this then, *please*, I implore you to be smarter next time.

And I do have one final note for my grandmother:

Jennie, having made your debut on TV and having revealed the cost of my house, causing me much embarrassment, you don't then come on my radio show and reveal that either you (or possibly your mum?) had a secret child – an uncle (or possibly great-uncle?) that neither your grandson (or possibly great-grandson?) or daughter (or possibly granddaughter?) ever knew about.

It pains me to say this but, since your death, Jennie, you have become nothing but a nuisance. So please – don't contact me through Sally again.

And Sally, if my grandmother does get in touch – please keep her thoughts, guesses and inappropriate financial revelations to yourself.

Sally. Thank you.

Chapter 5

THE CURIOUS CASE OF THE PERVERT MOST TERRIBLE

Are you familiar with sexual perversion?

I'm not trying to get off with you, I'm just starting a chapter dramatically.

A few weeks ago, a woman approached me in the Groucho Club.

It's a members' club in Central London that attracts people from the worlds of TV, film, music and drinking. And, on this night, it also admitted people from the world of sexual perversion (although if super-injunctions have taught us anything, it is that those two worlds are not mutually exclusive).

In the interests of not having my membership revoked, this was a one-off appearance by a sexual pervert in the otherwise entirely respectable Groucho Club (the Groucho Club is named after Groucho Marx because of his legendary witticism, 'I would never want to be a member of a club that didn't charge nearly £7 for a little drink).

There were warning signs that she was a sexual pervert.

Firstly, she was a woman with a lot of tattoos, which in my experience usually means anything goes. Secondly, she immediately began talking about having sex, which I have always found is a clear giveaway that someone's interested in having sex.

I began reviewing the evidence before me in the manner, I like to think, of Steven Moffat's creation, Sherlock Holmes.[11]

Tattoos. Talking about sex. Thigh-high shiny black leather boots tapering down to spiked heels. The fact that she was still talking about sex. Nose ring (exactly the same signifier as tattoos).

There was no doubt about it, Watson: this young lady was clearly of a disposition *most* sexually perverse.

It was as clear, dear readers, as the nose ring on her face.

(As an aside, I recently saw a gentleman perform a 'reverse Sherlock'. A cab driver in Edinburgh collected my friend and me at Waverley Station. My pal is likewise employed in the TV and radio industry.

This eagle-eyed cabbie scrutinised us in his rear-view mirror. He was very clearly analysing every minute detail in order to build up a picture of the precise nature of

---

[11] If you write me a letter saying, 'Steven Moffat didn't create Sherlock Holmes,' I will instantly and correctly deduce from that letter that you are simple.

these young (well, -ish) men in the back of his Hackney carriage. Taking in each individual clue in turn: the first-class tickets clasped in my right hand. My brand-new, rather flamboyant Vivienne Westwood blazer. Our soft, uncalloused hands, the aroma of Cowshed hand moisturiser, an £800 brand-new Globe-Trotter suitcase, which he'd personally loaded into the car after my friend's bag, which was the exact weight of an iPad, a MacBook Air and a copy of Jon Ronson's *The Psychopath Test*.

And there was one final clue that didn't escape his notice: as we drove past the Edinburgh Conference Centre my friend and I discussed a seminar we'd attended there for the Edinburgh Television Festival in which *Guardian* humorist Charlie Brooker had interviewed the creator of *The Wire*, David Simon.

Inspiration visited him suddenly. The breakthrough moment was upon him. Like Michael Faraday at the Royal Institution, he turned to his rapt audience and presented his findings: 'So, ye tae laddies just awf o' the rigs, eh?')

So, as I stood in front of this girl in the Groucho Club, I was determined to read the situation correctly.

And I had. She was a sexual pervert.

But even though I was fully aware of what she was, nothing could have prepared me for what she said next.

'Do you want any dom?'

And I couldn't have been prepared because I hadn't any idea what she meant. And I hope neither do you.

My first thought was that she might have meant Dom

Perignon champagne, but the way she said it made that seem unlikely.

'I'm so sorry,' I said, genuinely puzzled, 'I've absolutely no idea what you mean.'

'Dom. Dominatrix. I do domination.'

She was speaking words that I could hear but couldn't understand, like when someone says they are involved in corporate responsibility for HSBC Europe.

Although unlike with any job at HSBC Europe, I thought it would be interesting to find out what this job of hers entailed.

'You know what, I've heard the word dominatrix, but I don't really get it. I know it involves a woman being in a dominant position sexually, but other than that I don't know the ins and outs.' (That's not innuendo.)

She explained it as if I were an inquisitive child (under no circumstances explain this to an inquisitive child). Her eyes tightened. Her jaw clenched. Her fists tensed into little balls – I was already beginning to get a sense of what domination might be like.

She whispered into my ear, 'I stick my foot in your mouth, flick ash onto your face and hit you with a whip.'

'You're not really selling it to me,' I nervously replied. (Although technically she was selling it to me and presumably was hoping to quote a price).

Rarely have I heard anything that sounds less like my cup of tea. But I dare say, if I'd asked, she'd have been willing to push that cup of tea up my bottom. And then invoiced me.

We had a perfectly civil exchange, I thanked her for the 'kind offer' and bid her good day.

But in conclusion, I should stress for legal reasons that if you are that dominatrix woman I met in the Groucho that night, I've got absolutely no evidence that you've ever pushed a teacup up somebody's bottom.

Chapter 6

FIVE THINGS I HAVE LEARNED THAT YOU SHOULD NEVER DO

1) Never ever get a hot tub

I'm not proud to admit this but, between 2003 and 2007, I owned a hot tub.

I bought it from a showroom in Godalming in Surrey (whose famous residents include Ashley Cole and Alvin Stardust),[12] and I had it installed in the garden of the new-build modern mews house where I lived in Chiswick.[13]

All these biographical details might lead you to the conclusion that I have the taste and sophistication of an Autoglass League footballer. I don't. Or at least, I did.

I invested in one because in the cosiness of the

---

[12] Alvin would later go on to become a laugh-free punch line in my stand-up set (see Chapter Thirteen).

[13] See Number 2 in my list of things never to do.

showroom, with its water clear, warm and bubbling and the spotlights illuminating it, it looked quite nice.

But in the dark, damp, tiny paved yard behind my old (brand-new) house, which was overlooked by a pedestrian bridge crossing a busy railway, it didn't look nice at all.

It looked like a pond for people.

Let me tell you what I've learned from bitter experience: hot tubs are dreadful.

You buy them because they seem somehow sociable and aspirational. You imagine you'll be spending warm, sunny days and nights clambering into these hot tubs with a group of attractive friends. With cocktails and champagne on the side, the warm summer afternoon will give way to a balmy evening, with an undercurrent of perfect contentment and thrilling sexual possibility. One thing's for certain, you think: you'll be the envy of everyone who sees it.

It turns out that the one thing that is certain is that you'll never once achieve that scenario. Not once. The best you can hope for, is that your friends will think you're fucking weird if you try and get them in it. If they don't, then *they* are fucking weird and should be sacked off.

You have to think about it from the vantage point of the guests you expect to clamber in. You've never been to a dinner party and thought, 'Well, that was a wonderful evening – the food was delicious, the wine an excellent choice, and the conversation entertaining from start to finish. But do you know what would improve it? If the host invited me and my husband to strip down to our underwear and sit with him in a big outdoor bath (which he filled up with water *five weeks ago*) before we go home wet, shivering and stinking of chlorine.'

The only people who'd be interested in an evening that ends in a hot tub are the sort of people who'd also be interested in an evening that ends in swapping wives. And I do not want that sort of person coming to my house for dinner.

Well, you may be thinking, at least you could enjoy the hot tub when you're on your own.

No, you can't. A hot tub affords no enjoyment unless you are partial to buying box after box of a particular type of chlorine (which is both hard to source and expensive), installing new filters every fourth time you use it and draining all the filthy water out every three months because it's gone stagnant again.

For four years, a third of my tiny garden was dwarfed by a lump of plastic with all the aesthetic beauty of a child's paddling pool – only twice as big and without the option to dismantle it.

The idyllic setting was only enhanced by the up-to-sixteen trains passing per hour, shooting out the aroma of burning brakes and the near-constant screech of the metal wheels against the rails.

But if you've just read this and still fancy having all of these problems, they can be yours for a little over three grand (at the cheapest).

When I put the house on the market, I naively asked the estate agent if the hot tub would add any value to the property. He paused, looked concerned, and then said he didn't think the hot tub would *damage* the house's value per se, but it *would* put some buyers off. Even a man whose profession is barefaced lying is forced to tell the truth when confronted with a hot tub.

I decided not to add the entire cost of the hot tub onto the asking price of the house when it went on the market, but thought at the very least it would be a nice little extra for whoever bought my home. The free gift of a hot tub.

Wrong.

The man who bought my house refused to complete on his offer until I'd had it removed.

2) Never buy a really ugly modern mews house

Let me just clarify: I don't mean 'don't buy a modern mews house. Some are perfectly nice. I mean 'don't buy a really ugly modern mews house in Chiswick that's badly built and has a busy railway behind it.' And I specifically mean 'don't buy the really ugly modern mews house in Chiswick that's badly built and has a busy railway behind it . . . that I bought and lived in for four years.'

As a prize on the Capital Radio *Drivetime Show*, I once gave my house away to a listener for an afternoon. I was broadcasting from the studios in Leicester Square and we had a live link-up to the listener in my home.

On air, I asked this young lady what she thought of it.

She paused before quietly saying, 'Er . . . it's not really what I expected.' She then explained that it was so unpleasant she thought it was just some house we'd rented for the day, so she'd then started rooting through drawers to find evidence I lived there. She later told the producer off air that she thought my home was a 'shit hole'.[14]

I once locked myself out and it took a former member of the Kosovan army (who was then driving a Chiswick minicab) less than a minute to break in. He managed to open one of the flimsy UPVC windows in less time than it took to close one of the bloody things.

The same windows were once easily opened in the middle of the night by some kids, who jumped from the railway bridge into the back yard and clambered through the house while my girlfriend and I were sleeping upstairs.

We were woken by Barclays Bank's fraud prevention unit asking if we had been on a spending spree at petrol stations across West London. (They are quite thorough, the Barclays fraud prevention unit. They once called me to tell me that my card had been stolen as it had been used to pay a £700 bill at a branch of Hooters in Nottingham. 'Ah,' I said. 'Stand down, officers.')

---

[14] Actually there's a sixth thing I've learned you should never do: 'Never invite a listener to your house.' Sadly, I imagine this advice will fall on deaf ears in the television and radio presenting community, many of whom like nothing more than taking awestruck listeners and viewers, whom they've met at drunken corporate dos and charity auctions, back to their properties and then having sex with them. This also forms the seventh thing I learned you should never do: 'Never sleep with a listener.'

3) Never ask Bill Nighy a question

Back in 2005 I was at a BAFTA screening of a Richard Curtis film called *The Girl in the Café*. I can't quite recall what it was about – something to do with a chick meeting the Chancellor in a café and flirting with him until he cancels Third World debt.

Many years later, Italian premier Silvio Berlusconi would do *exactly* the same thing that Richard Curtis had imagined in this film, only without the bit where Third World debt was cancelled. And the chick wasn't a chick in a café; she was five prostitutes from an escort agency. Although I suppose there was some redistribution of wealth once they were done.

The BAFTA auditorium was rammed and I was sitting on a seat right on the end of a row. The room was dark and the film had already begun when Hugh Grant, the long-time Richard Curtis collaborator, turned up with his then-girlfriend, Jemima Khan.

Because the place was packed and the film had commenced, they had to sit on the steps at the side of the auditorium, right next to me.

I don't mind telling you that I initially found this rather exciting. Sitting next to Hugh Grant! At a screening of a Richard Curtis film! And he'd brought along Jemima. Pretty cool, I thought. But it wasn't cool. Or at least it didn't turn out that way.

As part of the screening, Richard Curtis took questions from the audience, along with the esteemed actor Bill Nighy, who played the Chancellor. (I think. It was a long time ago. He certainly didn't play the chick.)

Hugh Grant tapped me on the leg to introduce himself and tell me that Jemima had a burning question she wanted to ask. However, she didn't want to draw attention to herself, fair enough, so Hugh wanted to know if I would ask the question on her behalf. Totes. So Jemima began to brief me but took a while (the question was basically about the problem of Third World dictators personally pocketing aid money to spend on yachts and weaponry. Jemima didn't boil it down that concisely.)

Bill Nighy was looking over. And Bill Nighy was looking cross.

He clearly thought we were being disrespectful, nattering about dinner or something. Oh, how I wish we'd been talking about dinner (and the going-out-for-it of). We hadn't (although if we had then sure, I would have loved to. Offer still stands). We'd been talking about dictators. For ages. Bill shot me an angry glance, which was a tad unfair – I was simply following the protocols of politeness in such circumstances and really, should not have been stared at with anger by Bill Nighy. Or, for that matter, anyone in the cast of *The Girl in the Café* including, but not limited to, Kelly Macdonald, Ken Stott and Toshie Ogura (Toshie's not as famous as the others but, having checked IMDb, she played 'Japanese Delegate' in the film, which was a step up from her previous role as 'Japanese Woman' in Bill Murray's 1997 movie, *The Man Who Knew Too Little*).

Once Jemima had completed her fairly complex briefing, I raised my hand.

With some sort of sixth sense, my girlfriend, sitting on the other side of me, urgently told me to lower that hand.

But I could hardly tell her that I'm shallow, and OF COURSE I was going to do Jemima Khan a favour.

And anyway, the question had been asked in conjunction with *Hugh Grant*! At the screening of a Richard Curtis film!

Indeed, mere moments later, I was personally reenacting that opening scene to the Richard Curtis film *Four Weddings and a Funeral* – the one where Hugh Grant utters the word 'fuck' over and over again.

I was passed the radio microphone and politely asked Bill Nighy a subbed-down version of the question.

Bill Nighy then bollocked me in front of the entire room.

Now, I should state for the record that Bill Nighy is, as the friends we have in common have told me, warm, charming and full of good humour. I know that to be true. But on this occasion, he definitely bollocked me in front of the entire room.

He said I'd been talking since I'd arrived (not true), the question was lazy (half true), that I'd not been paying attention (three-quarters true) and that the issue I'd raised had already been addressed earlier in the session (probably one hundred per cent true).

The room fell silent and stared at me, as my girlfriend sank into her chair. Still, at least it was over. Only it wasn't. Bill was just getting into his stride.

For the rest of the evening, no one would make eye

contact with me. Not even Jemima Khan, whom I've always gallantly refused to name as the originator of the question.[15]

Since then, I've been terrified about ever having to talk to Bill Nighy again. I know, ordinarily he's a very nice guy. But I'm scarred. And scared. Scared that I'd ask him another perfectly reasonable question – 'Would you like a cup of tea or coffee before we get started on the interview, Mr Nighy?' – and he'd go beserk.

'I've already been asked if I want a cup of coffee. Why weren't you listening? I've said I don't want one. Do you know how much work goes into harvesting a coffee bean? Do you?'

It's strange to have one of the country's most respected actors as a bit of a nemesis. I'm sure Bill will be reading this book, so I would like to address him directly. You'll notice I've not used any questions.

Hi Bill, it's Richard here. Richard Bacon.

Look, I just wanted to clear the air. I'm sure you remember that whole Q&A misunderstanding that took place back in 2005, and now you know it's actually Hugh Grant and/or Jemima Khan's fault and not really anything to do with me. I was hoping we could let bygones be bygones. You know, smoke the

---

[15] And, even though I'd be well within my rights to do so, I will never name her. If the publisher accidentally left the name in, that's an unforgivable error on their part and I would appreciate it if you entirely forgot Jemima's implicit involvement in this upsetting story. I'm very much hoping to have a conversation with her in the future that may include, but is not limited to, dictators and dinner (offer still stands).

old peace pipe, bury the hatchet, call off the dogs. We're both professional people and life's too short not to get along.

It seems crazy[16] that we let things get this far out of control. So it's been my constant hope[17] that we can put this whole mess behind us. So many years of evolution[18] and boy![19] we're still rocking the boat![20]

All the best,
Richard.

Does that sound alright, Bill?

Shit, I've used a question. Here he goes again.

4) Never buy a watch off a bloke in the street

Here's a scenario I want you to picture.

Imagine you are walking down Chiswick High Road, off to get some shopping from Waitrose (other supermarkets are available, but not in Chiswick).

---

[16] Seems Crazy is not the name of a Bill Nighy film. You're thinking of *Still Crazy*, where he played Ray Simms (1998, IMDb rating: 6.8/10).

[17] Constant Hope is not the name of a Bill Nighy film. You're thinking of *The Constant Gardener*, where he played Sir Bernard Pellegrin (2005, IMDb rating: 7.5/10).

[18] Evolution is not the name of a Bill Nighy film. You're thinking of *Underworld: Evolution*, where he played the vampire king, Viktor (2006, IMDb rating: 6.6/10).

[19] Boy is not the name of a Bill Nighy film. You're thinking of *Astro Boy*, where he provided the voice of Dr Elefun (2009, IMDb rating: 6.3/10).

[20] Rocking the Boat is not the name of a Bill Nighy film. You're thinking of *The Boat That Rocked*, where he played Quentin (2009, IMDb rating: 7.4/10).

A bloke in a BMW 3 Series with blacked-out windows suddenly pulls over and tells you that he is on his way home from a 'Rolex convention' in Hammersmith and that he's got 'a couple of watches left over' that he can 'flog off' dead cheap.

Do you:

(a) Tell him that you have never heard of a Rolex convention, that you suspect such a thing doesn't even exist and that, even if they did, you doubt Rolex would tell their staff to flog them on the way home for whatever they can get (in this case, £70). An entry-level Rolex is a grand. Rolex go out of their way to associate themselves with the high end. Since 1905, when they started in London under the name Wilsdorf and Davis (registering the trademark name 'Rolex' three years later), the company have been synonymous with quality. In the entrance lobby to the most expensive real estate in the UK, called One Hyde Park, the *only* shop is a Rolex store (the novelty and usefulness of which must wear off amazingly quickly if you lived in one of the apartments. You'd never open the fridge and find you've run out of Rolex). Then turn your back on him, and whistle for a policeman.

Or

(b) Say, 'Seventy quid for a Rolex? That's incredible! Thanks so much. This scenario seems entirely convincing.'

I went for the latter.

The Rolex stopped after a day.

And I was furious, because you always hear about how reliable Rolexes are.

5) Never appear drunk on television

A few years back a couple of friends and I came up with a strange late-night TV show called *Flipside*. I don't mean 'strange' pejoratively. It was often great. But it *was* also strange.

Three guests would watch television and tell you what was happening on all the other channels. Think of it like a live TV comedy panel show.

It started out on the now long-dead cable channel Nation 217. Nation 217 sounds a bit racist. It wasn't – if anything, every night it showed how multicultural it was by allowing women of all colours to man phone lines in their bras and pants and talk to pathetic and lonely viewers.

The show was like a DVD director's commentary by a load of people who had nothing to do with making the shows, hadn't seen them before and often hadn't even heard of them. When it worked (which admittedly it didn't always), it was one of the most exciting shows to watch.

Both Justin Lee Collins and Karl Pilkington made their TV debuts on the show, which was on every night. I hosted it a couple of times a week and had begun to really relax into the job.

So much so that, with Christmas around the corner and a show later that evening, I went out for a boozy lunch with a load of Channel 5's commissioners and got carried away.

To cut a long story short (and to skirt over the fact that I don't remember much of it), I got really, properly, staggeringly drunk.

Typically, I'd argue, when hosting any live television show, you want to be at the studio a good two hours before transmission. When you are also technically in charge of that show (I was also co-executive producer), you should try and make it quite a bit earlier than that. On this drunken night, I arrived ten minutes *after* the show had gone on air.

To add to the panic in the studio, I was so drunk I wasn't answering my phone. So at the last minute (in fact it was during the ten-second countdown to going live), they made one of the panelists, Marc Haynes, into the main presenter.

The first time Marc ever laid eyes on a script for *Flipside*, he was reading it out. The autocue hadn't been updated and, in his first line, he introduced himself as Richard Bacon.

What I remember about my eventual appearance on the show has been cobbled together from other people.

I was more drunk than I have ever been.

When I got to the studio, the floor manager took one look at me, put his arm out and told me that I wasn't allowed on set. I told him that I outranked him, strode past him, collapsed into the vacant chair and demanded, on air, that someone bring me a beer.

When they went to an ad break, the runner told me I wasn't allowed that beer. I told him to bring me a beer immediately. In that state, I seemed to imagine I was a three-star army general rather than what I was, the exec of a low-rent show on a ropy racist-sounding TV channel.

One of the other guests was the presenter Jayne Sharp, best known for later becoming the second Mrs Comedy Dave. As we came back from an ad break, I slurringly asked her, 'Wha showz yooo prezentin' at the mome . . . mome . . . momen?'

She said she'd just moved from presenting an ITV1 show to host *Glory Ball Live* on Challenge TV. Marc filled the awkward silence by saying, 'Bit hard to dress that up as a *sideways* move.'

Because I was really tickled, not only did I keep chuckling for the next twenty minutes, I also kept shouting, 'Hard to dress up as a sideways move, a ha ha!' whenever Marc or Jayne spoke. Or the other guest spoke. Or when they all stayed silent – it didn't really matter to me by that stage.

The next day, I was made to personally call every single one of the production team and Jayne and apologise. And I meant it from the heart, even though I had absolutely no recollection of what I was apologising for.

So let's run through those five points one by one:

Point one: Never buy a hot tub.

Point two: Never buy One Percival Mews in Chiswick (I don't believe this was the advice I gave the person who bought it from me when they came to view it, but I'm sure it's a view they now hold).

Point three: Don't ask a question of Bill Nighy. But if he ever asks you if you think he should buy a hot tub or One Percival Mews in Chiswick, tell him to go ahead immediately.

Point four: Never buy a Rolex off a man in the street (if Bill Nighy ever asks you, tell him any Rolex you buy off a man in the street is fully guaranteed, and recent research has found they're actually *more* accurate than the ones you get in the stores).

Point five: Never appear drunk on TV (I'd make another mention of Bill Nighy here, but he's a recovering alcoholic so I will not).

Chapter 7

HOW TO WRITE A FILM COLUMN WITHOUT SEEING THE FILMS (OR WRITING THE COLUMN)

One of the greatest jobs in the world must surely be that of a film critic for a well-respected national newspaper.

I can't imagine what that job is like. I've never had a job like that.

But I did once work as *The People*'s film critic for five years.

How to describe *The People* newspaper? What can one say about *The People* that hasn't already been said?

Anything you like. Because nobody ever talks about it.

When journalists discuss endemic phone hacking, no one mentions *The People*.

When TV shows review the morning's papers, no one mentions *The People*.

When films put up quotes from the Sunday review pages, no one mentions *The People*.

And when the hotel receptionist asks, 'What paper do you want delivered in the morning, sir?' no one mentions *The People*.

It feels like the child in the family that everyone ignores – and yet *The People* is one of the country's oldest papers. Launched in 1881 its first headline was on the Jack the Ripper murders. Its crime reporting in the 1960s was fearless – it was the first paper to name the Krays. Since those heady days it has, admittedly, been a bit on the quiet side.

But it did have *one* major scoop in our lifetimes. It's no Watergate. And it's no MPs' expenses. It's better than both.

The actor Leslie Grantham had just returned to EastEnders attended by mammoth hype. Between scenes he was relaxing in his dressing room on the BBC's prestigious Elstree lot, having carefully memorised all of his lines (I reprint them here in their entirety: ''Ello Princess').

Leslie wanted to kick back, clear his mind and have a bit of 'me time' before he was due back on the set of the country's biggest soap opera. So he did what *any of us* would do in the circumstances.

He simulated sex dressed as Captain Hook to a sexually available middle-aged woman on a webcam.

Sadly this innocent scene wasn't all it was cracked up to be.

Poor Leslie Grantham had been misled. He wasn't talking to a sexually available middle-aged woman on a webcam. He was talking to a sexually available middle-aged heterosexual journalist from *The People*. But it *was* on a webcam.

This story was a high watermark in modern tabloid journalism.

In all my years working there, and in all the years since, I have *never* seen anyone actually buy *The People*. The only time I know for sure that someone bought it is via a friend who says she saw a lady in Devon with a copy under her arm (that claim has not been backed up by a second source).

I went to a newsagent in Richmond to buy a copy once. They had one. It was kept under the counter next to *Razzle*.

Having said that, I like *The People*. This runt child of the newspaper world. And I remember my time there with nothing but affection.

But how, you must be wondering after reading this chapter's title, does one write a film column without seeing the films, or writing the column, even in a paper like *The People*?

Well, let's deal now with the first half of that statement and I'll explain the second in due course. A magician must not reveal all of his secrets at once, you know.

(*The People* did once run a story about a magician;

he turned out to be a paedophile. I won't repeat the headline.)

When I started that job I did see all of the films and wrote all of the columns. My first review was of *Love Actually*, which I penned in a Top of the Pops dressing room – a venue that now seems rather remote from the cosy, charming world of Richard Curtis romantic comedies.

For a short period of time, I really enjoyed the job. Somewhere, around three weeks in, it dawned on me that seeing three films a week was a bloody drag. And most of them were crap anyway. This thought struck me on a Wednesday morning sitting in an underground screening room with two others watching *Good Boy!*, a film about a dog from space who comes down to befriend an orphaned child.

It's one thing going to see a film everyone is banging on about on a Friday night with your girlfriend. It's quite another being forced to watch *Anaconda 2* in the middle of a Tuesday afternoon. So I got my film enthusiast friend Marc involved.

For a few weeks we divided the screenings between us and wrote together. Then I got bored of the screenings but we still wrote together. So there you go, the secrets of the first half of the chapter's title (how to write a film column without actually seeing any of the films) have been given up. Gifted to you in a way they never were to either the management or the readers of *The People*.

Now you want Sherlock here to reveal the second half

of the mystery: how to *write* a column without *writing* it. Here you go then.

I got bored of writing the column with Marc and let him do it all. Dah-da!

It was still done under the name 'Bacon at the Movies' and we used to give the films 'Bacon rashers' out of five.

Marc then got bored of going to the screenings too, so he started reviewing the films based on stuff he found on the web. I know what you're thinking: this was a foolproof system. Dear readers, let me stop you there. It wasn't.

Having handed over the column, I made the critical error of no longer even reading the column that I had not been writing, while the person who was writing it wasn't watching the films he was writing about.

To recap: I didn't see the films. I didn't write the column. And in common with the rest of the country, I didn't read the column.

Although it turned out that *some people* in the country did read the column. Film PRs.

And it was one of those who would be my *Downfall* (four Bacon rashers).

One balmy Monday evening, the day after *The People* was published, I was scoffing some Japanese food at an outstanding London restaurant called Roka. As another piece of salmon sashimi slipped down my oesophagus, thoughts of lowbrow tabloid film reviews couldn't have been further from my mind.

I was about to be caught out by a piece of terrible *Serendipity* (two Bacon rashers, what *was* John Cusack thinking?) and my boat was about to be rocked. (My Boat Was About To Be Rocked is not the name of a film. You're thinking of *The Boat That Rocked*, where Bill Nighy played Quentin – (2009, IMDb rating: 7.4/10.)

A lady wearing an Alexander McQueen skull scarf and oversized Tom Ford sunglasses approached me. I vaguely recognised her and asked her what she was doing here. She was attending a party in the bar beneath Roka to celebrate the premiere earlier that evening of a film called *The Lakehouse*. She told me she was promoting *The Lakehouse*. I knew what she was talking about because I'd read a review of *The Lakehouse* – in a different newspaper.

'Ah, yeah,' I said, 'that's the one where they're living two years apart, isn't it?'

She nodded and told me that the film's stars Keanu Reeves and Sandra Bullock were downstairs in that bar. 'Cool!' I said, at this stage hoping for an invite, adding, I thought helpfully, 'and I'll definitely try and see *The Lakehouse*.'

'You've already seen it.'

I stared blankly back at her. This woman was crazy. I had not seen *The Lakehouse*.

'I don't think so,' I said in all sincerity.

'You wrote a review of it yesterday in a national newspaper,' she replied.

Ah. Ooh. I see what's happened here. There was no

point in trying to keep up the pretence. And what was the film PR going to do: tell Keanu and Sandra? I doubt either of them has *The People* delivered. I don't think anyone successful has *The People* delivered. The only people who seem to buy *The People* are those with an unhealthy interest in the Yorkshire Ripper. This was suggested by the fact that whenever *The People* stuck a story about the Yorkshire Ripper on the front cover, sales went through the roof.

'Do you want to know what you thought about it?' she asked me.

'Erm . . . yes.'

'You didn't like it very much,' she said sarcastically.

I shrank into my chair and thought the only way to make the best of a bad situation would be to admit defeat and play along.

'That's right,' I said. 'I didn't like it.'

She now adopted a deliberately patronising tone. 'And do you remember why?'

'It was too . . . long? . . . Short? . . . Complicated? . . . Simple?'

She didn't laugh, but raised her eyebrows so high they were visible over the top of her enormous Tom Ford sunglasses and, with that look, neatly conveyed disappointment, irritation and pity before walking off. It takes a lot to convey all that with a pair of eyebrows, and in that sense her performance was easily better than that of Keanu Reeves in *The Lakehouse*.

Don't take my word for it. Take *The People*'s film critic

Richard Bacon's word for it. Here's what I (well, Marc) wrote:

> It's taken twelve years, but finally, dear readers, the stars
> of *Speed* have been reunited! Keanu Reeves and Sandra
> Bullock, who set the box office on fire back in 1994, are
> back! And this time the bomb isn't on the bus it's up on
> the cinema screen and they're STARRING in it!

(You see I did *occasionally* read my own reviews. In this case six years after it was published in order to quote it in this book.)

I got done again while walking through Soho. A trendy-looking bloke in his late thirties (a *People* reader in disguise) sidled up to me and told me he was a director and that I'd negatively reviewed his film the previous weekend (if memory serves it was something to do with a bicycle ride to Brighton, but I didn't see it so I can't be sure). He wanted to know *exactly* why I didn't like his film.

He was very pleasant. I told him I wasn't prepared to get into the ins and outs of my review in the street, which sounded like the sort of thing a genuine film critic would say.

If he's reading this now, then I'm sorry. I shouldn't have been writing reviews of films I hadn't seen (although as I wasn't actually writing them, I technically wasn't). Anyway, as a gesture of goodwill, I'm now increasing the number of Bacon rashers awarded his film to four. So whatever that film was, it's now got four Bacon rashers, so make sure you watch it if it comes on the telly (don't know it's name, sorry).

The most upset the column ever caused was due to one of the handful of reviews I *did* write myself, although I didn't see the film it was about.

It was called *Ladder 49* and concerned a group of American firefighters. Its release came a few months after the British firefighters' strike of 2004.

Here's part of that review:

> This is a film about firefighters. Not the type we have in Britain, it's not a big drama about people standing by the roadside disputing pay and working conditions and giving a thumbs up to anyone who honks.

Four days later *The People* told me I had a sack of mail waiting for me. They claimed they had never had as big a response to anything before. Not even to that week's story about the Yorkshire Ripper. The letters – hundreds and hundreds of them – were exclusively from firefighters. Angry firefighters.

So I dedicated the next week's column, again, one I actually wrote, to the brave boys and girls in blue. And yellow. And fluorescent bits. And sometimes breathing apparatus.

> Bruce Jackson, a firefighter of fifteen years has written to say, 'Your comments are not appreciated, I expect

that you have never required the help of the fire and rescue service. How about stepping back in time to your *Blue Peter* days and spend some time with us training and see what our job is really like?'

Dear Bruce, *Blue Peter* wouldn't have me back under any circumstances. But I take your point on board.

An unidentified firefighter from Crewe's Brightwell Red Watch has this stinging rebuke. 'Richard, it is nice to know that you have such a high regard for the male and female firefighters in this country and think that all we do is stand by the roadside demanding more pay and better working conditions and waiting for the public to honk their horns. I am sure it's very nice for somebody like you, a C list celebrity, to earn the money that you do and to be able to waste it on recreational drugs, but that is not the case for us.'

Hang on, unidentified firefighter from Crewe's Brightwell Red Watch. There's no need to be mean.

And Rob Nisbett from Oldham Greenwatch has written, 'Richard, I would be interested to know how much *you* would have to be paid to run into a burning building to search for someone or cut someone out of a car.'

Dear Rob, thank you; however, that would be a matter for my agent. I *never* discuss fees.

Anyway, the column that week was meant to be about *Meet the Fockers* which, because of the apology, I reviewed in a single throwaway line at the end of the column: 'Tiresome, disappointing, with a script as lazy as all of this country's nurses.' This in turn created another complaint – not from the nurses, but from the PR people for *Meet the Fockers*.

To say I took the whole experience a bit lightly would be bang on the money – but then so did *The People*. They allowed Marc to submit three drawings of monkeys instead of a review of *King Kong*. We realised that not only did I not read the column, but *The People*'s sub-editors – the guys who lay out the page and edit the copy down – weren't reading it either. Marc sent them some work over with notes in brackets asking them to fact-check something he'd written. So *this* sentence was printed 800,000 times, distributed around the country by lorry to newsagents from Lossiemouth to Padstow: 'Subs, can you check that line please? Don't want any legal issues, nice one.'

And here's the thing: *no readers appeared to notice*.

It's like that famous philosophical question: if a tree falls over in the forest and there's no one to hear it, does it make a sound? I believe the answer to be no. Now let's take that one stage further. If someone then took that tree, dragged it to a lumber mill, pulped it and turned it into paper on which *The People* was printed, not only would it not have been heard, it wouldn't have been seen either.

Lesson learned. I would never put my name to reviews of films I didn't see ever again.[21]

---

[21] I did exactly the same thing a year later by becoming the film columnist for *Loaded* magazine, using an identical modus operandi.

To close, here is a review Marc and I wrote together. Our only ever review in verse. You'll read this and think, 'If *only* I'd had a bit of an obsession with stories about the Yorkshire Ripper about six years ago, I might have stumbled across this review on page 82 of the *Sunday People*, next door to the sex advice column.'

The Cat in the Hat, Fantasy, Cert: PG

Based on a kids' book by the late Dr Seuss,
This high-octane picture soon runs out of juice.
The pace is frenetic, the colours are blazing,
But *The Cat in the Hat* is far from amazing.
The problem, dear readers, is one thing just tires:
The schtick from the normally brilliant Mike Myers.
He's usually great and incredibly funny
But this time he's thinking, 'I'll just take the money.'
Two hours with Mike may seem very attractive
But in this he ain't funny, he's just hyperactive.
The costume, they claim, is made from real hair
But it looks more like something you'd win at a fair.
I'll be balanced, this isn't a critical mauling:
Some kids will enjoy it, some will think it's appalling.
It isn't the worst flick, but nevertheless,
This film is a massive great pile of cat mess.
Be warned that when it starts to play in your town
It's one hat-wearing cat you'll WANT to put down.

The PR also made a complaint about that one.

Chapter 8

THE TWEET THAT CHANGED EVERYTHING

For more than three years I have debated the merits of Twitter with all kinds of naysayers.

I have debated them on the radio, I have debated them in the street and I have debated them with my own family.

Again and again I have heard them bleat about it being 'a pointless load of old crap', before thundering out the most tiresome of clichés: 'Twitter. It's just celebrities spouting on about what they had for lunch.'

To which my response, without exception, was 'Bollocks.' Unless you're a caller to my Radio 5 Live show, in which case I thank you for your opinion, for which, of course, I have nothing but respect.

I decided that if you didn't like Twitter I had no time for you. I felt like Galileo having to nod along and bite my tongue as callers told me how the earth was the centre of the universe.

The person I bickered and feuded with more than any other on the topic of Twitter was my mother.

Until this point she had never changed her mind about anything, or admitted that she had ever been wrong . . . about anything.

We'd sit down and over a glass of wine would angrily and impatiently talk across one another as she laid into Twitter and all who sailed in her (posted stuff) as I imperiously listed its triumphs and victories.

'Hold it right there, Mum! What about the oppressed 2009 Iranian revolutionaries to whom Twitter gave a voice? And the thousands outside the country who changed their location to 'Tehran' in an act of global solidarity? Moving. Really bloody moving.'

As usual she wouldn't take in a word, instead barking out, 'I don't *care* what Stephen Fry is eating for dinner!'

I'd tell her about that fella convicted for making a joke about blowing the Robin Hood Airport 'sky high' if it closed in the snow and prevented his girlfriend from flying in. 'Thousands of people,' I cried, 'thousands of them, in support of his arrest and subsequent criminal record, retweeted his comments with the hashtag 'IAmSpartacus'. Stirring!'

'If I want to see what Duncan Bannatyne is having for brunch, I'll go to the fucking Ivy myself!' If mum *had* gone on Twitter at that time she'd have known Duncan Bannatyne is actually a Wolseley man.

I'd passionately rehearse the details of the moment Jan Moir, the *Daily Mail* columnist, was held to account by thousands of tweeters for writing her deeply insensitive article on the death of Stephen Gately, adding, 'Isn't that wonderful? And far from pointless.'

Mum would dismiss it all with a wave of the hand, grumbling that 'I couldn't care less what Alan Sugar thought of the buffet supplied for the Viglen team-building exercise of 2009!' (He actually thought it was pretty good: 'mouthwatering crispy prorns OK #PRORNS'.)

And so it went on.

'Mum, remember that guy, the one who tweeted from a Pakistani village having had a ringside seat at the assassination of Osama Bin Laden – and hadn't even realised it? Pretty thrilling, right?'

Again, nothing went in.

'And I don't even know who Michelle Dewberry is!' (She won the 2006 series of *The Apprentice*. 'So why would I care what she ate for her tea?' (Again, her 2009 tweet, also from the Viglen team-building exercise shows she also very much enjoyed the prawns: '#PRORNS').

There were so many other examples I lobbed her way. Anthony Weiner, the US Congressman, who attempted to send a picture of his penis via direct message to a 21-year-old female student and accidentally sent it to everyone.

Or how about the day my friend tweeted a picture of an RAC man who was interviewed on Sky News in December and had the world's greatest name, Crackers Patel?

Pointless load of old crap? Don't be daft.

For one of our later rows I'd even prepared a little

speech (the topic would come up so regularly). I stamped the wine glass back onto the table, drew myself up and thundered:

'Far from being trivial, dear mother, Twitter has empowered the oppressed, shone a light into murky corners and given a voice to the dispossessed [in my head I thought I sounded like the then-little-known Senator Barack Obama in his name-making 2004 speech to the Democratic Party Conference. The one where he said, 'We are not a collection of red states and blue states, we are the *United* States of America!']. Twitter has been at the vanguard of a global accountability revolution. [Bit pompous, sure.] The powerful can't get away with stuff unchecked anymore. From MPs' expenses to the banking crisis, from phone hacking to police bribery and the Arab Spring, Twitter – that's right – TWITTER was there, playing a significant part and thus making our world a better place!'

(I'm not sure it had anything to do with MPs' expenses, but mum didn't notice that inaccuracy.)

And then.

Then I saw the tweet that changed everything.

It was a tweet from my mother's dog.

You see, at some point my message had clearly cut through. I imagine it was when I told her about Crackers Patel.

She *had heard* what I had to say about the power of Twitter to change the world.

And my mother decided that this powerful tool,

untameable by dictators and democracies alike, would be the ideal platform to write fictional first-person tweets in which she pretended to be her dog. A Tibetan terrier called Bella.

Her Twitter handle is @BellaTheTibetan. Ironically, giving out this address will make it more popular and underscore her impression that tweeting first person as your dog is a wonderful thing.

Here's an example of one of her dog first-person tweets:

> Been walking in the rain, so my big Tibetan terrier paws are muddy, mum sez she is going for shower, so me is going with her (dad mustn't know).

Couple of quick observations about this tweet. Firstly, the dog sometimes appears to fully understand the first person pronoun 'I', and at others goes with the more pidgin 'me'. The dog character is inconsistent.

Secondly, she appears to be taking the dog into the shower with her. Something which, by saying 'dad mustn't know', she has clearly done on previous occasions and been told not to.

And thirdly, Mum, if you don't want Dad to know you are taking the dog into the shower, don't get the dog to tweet about it.

Sometimes the dog gets angry with members of my own family about events it didn't even attend. It's very critical of my sister Helena for not allowing it to come to her flat for a Christmas drinks do.

It has also, contacted Fenton (the dog that posh man chased after in Richmond Park that became a YouTube sensation). You might think, as a fellow dog, the two would get on. Not a bit of it. It turns out that Bella is insanely jealous of Fenton's popularity.

> @FentonTheDog I do dream in life of being followed by hundreds of people – don't happen to everyone – don't happen to me #YouJustLucky'.

That one was posted at two minutes past midnight.

The dog also entered into a brief correspondence with the comedienne Miranda Hart after Miranda said 'Missing Strictly already.' The dog replied 'Me too, woof!'

My mum is actually very bright; she doesn't tweet pidgin English on her own Twitter account. So therefore, she has deliberately given the dog baby-talk. And that's because if a Tibetan terrier were able to speak and type English, it wouldn't be able to speak and type *fluent* English. Of course.

It turns out *lots* of women do this. Oh yes, my mum is not the only woman tweeting as her dog. There are hundreds and hundreds of them. I know this because I had a look at some of the conversations my mum has had as *her* dog with other women tweeting as *their* dog.

Take @RubyBeagle. Her Twitter profile picture is of Ruby the beagle's head superimposed onto a bride.

Dame Ruby [she's ennobled her own dog] wishes it to be known that she is certainly not a racist as she likes Black and Chocolate Labs as much as Yellow! (I can only assume that someone has accused her dog of being bigoted.)

At Christmas Mum tweeted as her dog Bella, that 'Mummy' hadn't opened that day's door on the advent calendar:

It's 10.45am and not opened today's advent window. If she's not done it by 11am, gonna jump on kitchen worktop and get it myself!

Which means that Mum must have sat down in her kitchen, seen that the advent calendar window in front of her was not open for that particular day and, rather than reaching over and opening it herself she went online (she only tweets from her computer, which is in another room altogether) and wrote a tweet about it first-person from her dog.

And that one right there – *that* was the tweet that changed everything.

Mum, you have won the argument.

Congratulations.

Twitter is a pointless load of old crap.

Chapter 9

CHILDREN IN NEED (OF AN AMPHITHEATRE)

For the past few years I have been co-hosting a benefit gig.

I work at the same event, for the same charity, every year.

I know what you're thinking – 'Richard, you are a hero. The selfless giving of your time to help others is noble and inspirational. We admire you and wish we were more like you'.

That's only a natural sentiment.

And, dear reader, when you hear what cause the fundraising is for, that feeling will only be enhanced.

The event is called the House Festival and it takes place in the landscaped, manicured gardens of the 17th-century Chiswick House in West London. It's amazing. It is the best event of the year. Flawlessly organised, with first-class entertainment throughout the day, it makes Glyndebourne look like the Somme.

It began five years ago with the stated aim of raising funds to restore the open-air amphitheatre. It's situated in the Orange Tree Garden.

It's perhaps the only charitable event where you're raising money for people more fortunate than yourself.

Oh, I can almost hear you now: 'in a world of so much suffering and inequality, is raising money so that the people of a middle-class London suburb can see open-air productions of *Seven Brides for Seven Brothers* really the best use of your energies?'

Let me be clear. Yes. It. Is.

For too long now, the people of Chiswick have been denied one of their basic human rights: to see touring productions performed in venues without a roof.

This madness has to end. And it has to end soon.

Take a moment to think about twelve-year-old Allegra. She would dearly like to see an open-air production of *The Mikado*. And sure, she can – but why should she have to travel *all the way* to Windsor?

And what about eighty-four-year-old Edna? Her dying wish is to see *An Orchestral Tribute To The Music of Irving Berlin* being ruined by the rain in her immediate neighbourhood.

And it's not just me backing this charity. Some of the country's biggest stars also took a brave stand.

Ant and Dec co-host, Mumford & Sons and Lana Del Rey have performed, and so has Mark Ronson, who brought Jay-Z and Beyoncé with him.

That's right, even two of the America's brightest stars were moved by the plight of open-air theatre fans living in a posh London suburb.

Beyoncé wasn't scheduled to sing that night – and she didn't (I think she was too choked up.) But I reckon she wanted to let the people of Chiswick know that the world was thinking of them, was reaching out to them, and was praying for them.

As I stood on the stage and looked over the crowd of campaigners – a sea of Cath Kidston picnic rugs, Marc Jacobs scarves, and Chanel's limited-edition Particulair nail polish – I felt a lump come to my throat.

Not just because of the seemingly endless battle to restore the amphitheatre (it's been few years of fundraising and it doesn't seem to be ready yet) but because I was making a difference to the world.

My granddad was involved in D-Day and fought bravely and courageously against the Nazi menace. Well, on the day I hosted the House Festival in Chiswick this summer, I did something similar.

I stood up for something I believed in.

When my grandchildren ask me how I made the world a better place, I will produce some tickets for a performance of *A Midsummer's Night Dream* that's taking place in the garden of a historical house in W4.

And while we sit shivering on the uncomfortable seats, the actor's voices lost in the wind and a cloud of mosquitoes attacking us, I will say to them: 'This, children – this is what I did.'

Instantly, their eyes will well up with tears.
And I'm almost positive they will be tears of pride.

Chapter 10

IT'S NEW YEAR'S EVE, NOT NEW YEAR'S STEVE

I don't like anniversaries. Bad things always happen to me on anniversaries. Every. Single. Time.

It was on the tenth anniversary of *The Big Breakfast* that I, the host, found out that the show was being canned.

It was on the fifth anniversary of my film column that the *The People* threw me a surprise sacking.

And to mark *Blue Peter*'s fortieth I went on their summer expedition to several pages of the *News of the World*.

But recently, I discovered that celebrations don't just go wrong. Sometimes, they very nearly almost go right. And that's why I want to focus this chapter on multi-party sex sessions.

Let me begin by making a full and frank disclosure: I've never had one before. Not of any permutation. The most people in a bed when I've been performing sex has been two. From time to time, that figure's even dipped as low as one.

As the years passed and not a single group-sex frenzy came my way, I was starting to wonder if they were nothing more than a fable. As mythological as the massage with a happy ending (no one's ever had one. Ever. *That's a fact.*[22]

If anything, the idea confuses me. Twelve limbs in a single bed. It sounds like a logistical nightmare. Where do all the feet go? (Don't think I'm interested in feet, I'm not.)

And as I understand the mathematical arrangements, it sometimes involves another bloke. As a heterosexual man, inadvertent sexual contact with another bloke that I've only just met doesn't float my boat.

This is one of the few situations in life where it's seen to be beneficial to have the involvement of a complete stranger.

If you were purchasing a house you wouldn't ask a bloke you'd met in a nightclub if he wanted to co-own it with you while desperately trying not to stare up his bottom.

You wouldn't start a new media business with some dude you bumped into coming out of the pub, and work out monthly staff costs while your penises occasionally jangled together.

And you'd never hire a senior male solicitor for the

---

[22] If you have, you're a liar.

transfer of a land deed if there was a good chance that at some point his genitals might flop into your mouth.

Multi-party sex sessions truly had no appeal to me.

And then, a few months ago, *everything* changed.

I was at a party at a large country hotel celebrating New Year's Eve. All walled gardens, orchards, ormolu clocks and pheasant shooting. It was late. We'd been drinking. Everyone had headed to bed – apart from my wife, the renowned *Times* restaurant critic Giles Coren and a particularly good-looking couple we'd only just met. The lady half of that couple was a very friendly lingerie model called Gemma.

Around four that early winter's morning, Gemma suggested the five of us go swimming. And not just regular swimming, she laughed. Swimming, as the French would say, 'sans clothes' (I don't know the French word for clothes, sorry).

Restaurant critic Giles was salivating at the sight of the dish forming tonight's menu. He threw me a look that said, 'Ooh, we're about to see some nice breasts.' And that look was right. If anything, that look had slightly underestimated just how nice those breasts would turn out to be.

As we bobbed up and down in the water, it dawned on me that all the constituent parts for a multi-player sex fest were in place: it was the middle of the night, we were drunk, nude and sopping wet. And naturally, I thought to myself, 'God, are you sending me a message?'

Had He finally noticed Richard Bacon's life was barren

of threesomes and, as I had complained not, decided to lay on a special *fivesome* to make up for lost time? Was He telling me that the hour had come to put away childish things and become a man?

I folded my hands in prayer. 'Lord,' I whispered at the ceiling, 'if this be Thy will, I shall not let You down. I'm ready to do Thy bidding. And I'll start with Gemma. Thanks.'

Yet though God be perfect, man is not. At this very moment, Giles decided he was going to attempt (as he explained the next day) a 'closer look at Gemma's women's area'. (Giles didn't say the phrase 'women's area' – he'd be furious to see such an absurd and damply PC phrase attributed to him – but this is my book and I'm not having the filthy word Giles used printed in it. Save it for your sailor friends, Coren. Oh, and it wasn't the C-word. Somehow he found one even more unprintable than that.) The refracted light in the water had apparently made it tricky for Giles to see the fount of Gemma's womanly mystery (again, this wasn't what Giles called it) so he clambered out of the pool and dived back in, hoping to get a better view. I believe this is the first ever time that a literal 'muff-dive' had taken place in England. If English Heritage or any historians are reading this and know otherwise, do get in touch.

In his capacity as a restaurant critic, Giles had made his way through many an amuse-bouche. Now he was going off-menu, and he wanted something different. He wanted an amuse-vagina (I don't know the French word for vagina, sorry).

But then . . . disaster.

The mixture of Bordeaux, champagne and giddy school-boy excitement meant Giles's dive went spectacularly wrong. He missed his target, entering the water like a Westminster-School-educated lawn dart, smacking his nose on the base of the pool, coming up gasping for air and with a face covered in blood. He had also lost both contact lenses, which in many ways for him was a saving grace, as it meant he couldn't see the aghast looks on the faces around him. What a dozy woman's fount of all mystery (again, this isn't quite what Gemma's fella called Giles, but it's close enough).

My good friend Giles might have battered his nose, but he'd also battered my chances of breaking my duck. If a multi-party sex session had ever been on the cards, it certainly wasn't now.

Moments later, the very friendly but now dumbfounded lingerie model and her partner made their excuses and went off to bed, leaving me with my wife, and Giles with a swollen schnozz. I think Giles might have been hoping we could still kick off a threesome (he'd lost a lot of blood, his judgement was all over the shop), but considering it just involved my wife (with whom I have had sex plenty of times) and a man with a head injury, the idea didn't really appeal.

In the end, the only position I was now considering wasn't sexual: it was my previously held conviction.

Multi-party sex sessions are a stupid idea. They're a mess.

And God, what were You thinking? You should know better. You pervert.

Chapter 11

PLATE SPINNING BOB GOES TO VEGAS

A little while ago, I took part in a debate at the Oxford Union. I can't remember what the motion was exactly, but it was something along the lines of:

> *This House thinks that the media is a devalued profession.*

That was certainly the gist.

It pre-dated the Leveson Inquiry so a lot of people would have come with an open mind.

Apart from unsuccessfully trying to cop off with the then-president of the Oxford Union – the *Daily Mail* described her as 'the Asian Margaret Thatcher' – the only thing I recall is that my opponents, all of them media employees, seemed mortified by their own job.

One of them was Alan Rusbridger, the editor of *The*

Guardian. One of the most senior people in British media, as I remember he was only too keen to do it down.

I didn't like this sentiment and I'm not convinced he really meant it.

So I took him on.

There's a default position among a few in the media of claiming to be embarrassed by your job, while actually really enjoying your job.

It only comes out when they are talking to people who don't work in the game. To one another they wouldn't say it because they know it is, by and large, a bit of a jolly.

So once Alan had shut up, I rose to my feet, gripped the lectern and gave a stirring and emotionally charged speech about the industry. I implored these unworldly, guileless, starry-eyed Oxford undergraduates to tear up their plans for a career in the civil service or at an investment bank, or in medicine or the field of science, and instead talk on the radio. Or make some telly. Or try and get a short film off the ground. Or work in the music biz.

When I was listing media jobs I purposely left off 'work at *The Guardian*' because I don't know what it's like to be employed there and one of these eager students could have heeded my words, got a gig at the paper and found themselves spending their days writing articles about 'The Ecological Impact of the Rising Prices of Quinoa'. And I could never have that on my conscience.

I concluded my oration with an impassioned invocation: 'Come on in, the water's lovely!'

I won't assume you're familiar with the Oxford

debating chamber. It looks a little like the House of Commons and, after each debate, the students file out through one of two doors. Either the one with 'AYES' written above or the one with 'NOES'.

As I watched those bright little munchkins make their way through the AYES and NOES, I wondered if I'd done enough. Would this vote go my way?

I wanted to win and I was pretty sure I was on the right side of the argument. Again, it was pre Leveson.

The odds were stacked against me. On one side there was Alan Rusbridger, a man who led the 2011 investigation into phone-hacking, which had made journalistic history as well as courageously breaking the story of WikiLeaks to the world – on the other a man who, that afternoon on Capital Radio, had given a pair of Maroon 5 tickets to Stacey from Lewisham for doing a impression of a pig.

They said it couldn't be done.

They said there's simply no way Richard Bacon's oratory and mastery of subject could outsmart and out-argue the darling of the left, Alan bloody Rusbridger.

Well *they* were wrong.

Sure, it was by the narrowest of margins. Sure, but for the views of just a couple of the audience, history would have recorded a different verdict.

But it didn't.

And the narrowness of the victory doesn't matter in the slightest because in a democracy a majority – however slim – is a majority. In my little world it felt like a version of some landmark election victory: Aung San Suu Kyi's 2012 election to the Burmese parliament, the triumph of trade union leader Lech Walesa, made president of Poland in 1990, or the 1979 victory of Margaret Thatcher (not the Asian one).

So, in one of the oldest and most august debating chambers in the land, addressed in its time by the Dalai Lama, Nelson Mandela and Geri Halliwell, I had taken on one of the sharpest journalistic minds of his generation – and I HAD WON![23]

The reason I had won (do read that footnote) was because I meant it.

I have enjoyed, indeed usually loved, more or less every media job I've had. Like all proud parents, I pretend I don't have a favourite and love all of them equally. But like all proud parents, I secretly think one of them stands head and shoulders above the rest. Certainly in terms of fun.

The Big Breakfast.

Back in 1998, after that terribly silly sacking business a few ropy offers immediately came my way.

Ropiest amongst them was Talksport, which offered me twenty grand to host their *Breakfast Show* for a single week. Sadly, after a meeting with the bosses, I was

---

[23] I later found out that the member of the Oxford Union responsible for counting had taken a shine to me and had fiddled the vote in my favour. I'd actually lost. But only *just*. And in a democracy, a near victory is as good as a victory. I can't remember who that member of the Oxford Union was. Not the Asian Margaret Thatcher. A different one (not a different *Asian*, although, that said, it could have been because it wasn't someone I fancied so I have no recollection of them). Anyway, thanks, mystery corrupt chick.

told my 'low-to-medium levels of sexism' fell below the required standard.

The radio station Atlantic 252 also came calling, with an offer so tempting that today I have absolutely no recollection of whatever it was they offered me. There were opportunities to appear on *TFI Friday* and the Virgin *Breakfast Show* with Chris Evans, which in any other circumstances I would have done in a heartbeat.

But my PR man, Stuart Higgins, told me to lie low. At the time of writing, Stuart is handling the PR for Oscar Pistorius. Stuart must look back fondly on those innocent, simple days, when all he had to do was get a drug-using *Blue Peter* presenter back on the telly.

Without his cautious advice and mentoring, I don't think I'd have a career today.

Even worse, I might have one on Talksport.

I had a few months out of work with nothing to do and not a great deal on the horizon.

And then, I was offered a job on Channel 4's *The Big Breakfast*.

If *Blue Peter* was like a very traditional British public school, then *The Big Breakfast* was akin to a sixth-form college for mouthy, like-minded, eccentric, creative, slightly flawed kids who were living away from home for the first time.

The job they'd given me involved knocking on random folks' doors live on the telly at seven in the morning. You might remember that Mark Lamarr and Keith Chegwin also did stints at this job.

For my inaugural outside broadcast, I was sent to Liverpool to front a feature called 'Bringing Home the Bacon'. With *all Big Breakfast* features the title came first and the content followed limply in its wake. I desperately needed it to go well because the show's presenter and spiritual leader, Johnny Vaughan, tended to make snap decisions about whether he liked you or not. And if didn't like you, he'd let you know, and immediately after he'd let the viewers know.

Our little team left the local Travelodge in the pitch black and headed to the location – a cul-de-sac of modern, Brookside-style housing. One of the families had been nominated by their friends, and we were here to surprise them at the break of dawn – with a plate spinner.

That surprise essentially boiled down to a family groggily wondering why on earth there was a plate spinner in their garden at seven-fifteen in the morning.

'Plate Spinning Bob', his professional name, arrived just after six. I'm sure he won't mind me telling you this, but he exuded an air of complete ineptitude. He popped open the boot of his car and peered inside and I watched as an inept look of inept dismay ineptly flashed across his inept little face.

'Ah . . .' muttered Bob

His hesitancy made it perfectly obvious something wasn't right.

'What is it, Bob?'

'I've forgotten my plates.'

'You've forgotten your what, Plate Spinning Bob? You

had just two things to remember, didn't you, Bob? Two things. Sticks. And plates. Sticks and plates.'

So a man with a handy aide-memoire built into his *own name* had forgotten fifty per cent of the kit he needed to do his job.

The only option available to us, apart from smashing the sticks across Bob's face (he was too likable for that), was to find some bloody plates. We knocked on the door of a neighbouring family (it was still before seven), told them we were from the telly and asked them for all their plates. This, I thought, was a tall order. These weren't plates we wanted to *borrow*. These plates – plates they were probably about to use for their breakfast, plates they'd probably also require for lunch and later at dinner – were going to be handed over to an inept plate spinner. Those plates weren't coming back.

But I was entirely wrong about it being a tall order, and I learned a valuable lesson that day – people really are happy and willing to do *anything*, just so long as it's at least tangentially related to the television.

If someone came to your door before sunrise, woke up your whole family and said they needed to destroy all your plates as a matter of urgency, you'd tell them to clear off. But if someone came to your door before sunrise, woke up your whole family and said they needed to destroy all of your plates as a matter of urgency *live on Channel 4* – you'd not only point out the cupboard they were sitting in, you'd carry those plates out of your house with a spring in your step and a song in your heart.

So we finally had the plates. But as Matt, the producer, reached for his walkie-talkie to inform base we were back on track, we learned *another* valuable lesson – a fascinating fact about plate spinning that I bet you don't know. We certainly didn't.

Plate spinning cannot be done with normal plates.

Plate spinning, said plate spinner Plate Spinning Bob, can only be performed with plates that have a pre-existing, precision-drilled indentation in the centre of the base of the plate.

So they're not so much 'plates' as 'specifically engineered china disks manufactured solely for use in spinning'. And, as such, they are not easy to find at six-fifteen in the morning in a cul-de-sac in Liverpool.

We went into the neighbour's garage, where they happily lent us their drill (I refer you to my earlier comments about being 'from the telly') and we made the indentations. Even if they didn't get smashed, they were already ruined.

Bob took one of the newly chiselled plates in his right hand and, in the only point of the experience where he looked remotely professional, started to feel its weight, raising and lowering it a little. A look of concern slowly spread across that little face: 'These are 'eavier than me normal plates.' All we could do was pray.

When we finally broadcast the feature live on Channel 4, from the garden of the family we'd originally planned to surprise, watched over by our specially invited guest, the leader of Liverpool City Council, every single plate, one after another, fell off the sticks onto the family patio and shattered into dozens of tiny pieces.

It was spectacular.

On *The Big Breakfast*, an on-air disaster was more warmly received than an on-air triumph. And via total disaster, in the ironic world of that programme, a non-plate-spinning star was born.

The jubilant boss, Ed Forsdick, immediately commissioned a follow-up – 'Plate Spinning Bob Goes to Vegas'.

The tape of 'Plate Spinning Bob Goes to Vegas' is the only tape of anything I've ever made that I've actually kept. Johnny Vaughan claims to still watch it regularly.

To pull off Ed's vision, I had to place a call to the legendary Circus Circus hotel on the Strip – and it turned out that one of the most famous entertainment venues in America can be seduced in exactly the same way as a neighbour in a modern cul-de-sac in Liverpool: just tell 'em it's for the telly.

The manager of Circus Circus was only too happy to welcome us (he'd probably also have given us his plates if we'd asked), but he had one strict criterion – any talent performing on his stage had to be world class. So how to get around this thorny issue?

Lie.

I explained that I was flying over an exceptionally talented plate spinner who'd been an enormous hit on 'England's biggest breakfast show'. The manager sounded genuinely excited and offered us a one-off spot on their main stage.

Plate Spinning Bob, or more accurately Six Empty Sticks Bob, was heading for the big time.

I remember the flight being long. My plate-spinning small talk proved to be quite limited. But I'll never forget Bob beaming as he saw the Strip for the first time in his life. Since childhood Bob had dreamed of Vegas but had never been able to afford to go. Now his unique talent had brought him here. It was lovely to see.

We checked in to Circus Circus and, as we stepped into the lift, Bob broke some news. I'd like to say this was a neatly thought out callback by my new friend. But it wasn't.

With our ears popping as we whistled up to the 1450th floor, that slow look of concern spread across his face once more.

'I meant to tell you, I haven't brought any plates.'

He hadn't *forgotten* them this time, he explained; he just thought they'd weigh too much to bring with him. Not an unreasonable point, but he could have mentioned it sooner. But being young and devious, the producer Dave and I knew that this presented us with a wonderful opportunity.

We told Bob *we'd* go and buy him some plates. In no time at all Dave and I were in a massive homeware store that stocked plates of all weights, sizes and circumferences. It took some rooting around, but we found exactly what we were looking for. The *heaviest* plates they had.

Now, we were just twenty-four hours from curtain

up – actually there was no curtain, the stage was in the centre of the room, but you get my drift. The Circus Circus hotel, an internationally famous cabaret venue, which had featured in an iconic scene in *Diamonds Are Forever*, sees artists performing at the limits of human capability day in, day out, and was about to welcome into its headline arena the glitter-covered, waistcoat-wearing, perspiration-drenched and completely incompetent Plate Spinning Bob.

I watched as excitable families poured into the arena – as it was the middle of the Easter holidays, every seat was taken. I nipped backstage, placed a hand on Bob's shoulder and wished him good luck before walking onto the stage myself to introduce him. I wanted to give Bob the biggest build-up I could muster.

'People of America! He has taken Britain by storm! He is here in Vegas for one performance only! You are about to witness history!'

They were going mad.

'He will only come out if you say after me: Bob! Bob! Bob!'

The venue filled with the harmonious chants of the name of a plate spinner whose last gig before getting on the plane had been at the Forest Care Residential Home in Eccles.

I had wound the crowd up to the point where they were almost screaming for him to come on stage.

'Ladies and gentlemen,' I said finally, 'please welcome Plate Spinning Barrrrrrrbb!!!'

He paused in the wings, taken aback by the roar of the biggest crowd he'd ever heard in his life.

He walked out, tentatively at first, and scanned the crowd. As one, they were beaming, whooping and applauding.

Bob smiled disbelievingly. He had that look of awe you see on a child's face when they unwrap their main present on Christmas morning: a mixture of joy, shock and just a touch of being overwhelmed.

As he stepped out onto the stage, his nerves evaporated, and he smiled back at them, clasped his hands and took a small bow. Those Vegas folk cheered *with even more vigour.*

I have often wondered if this was the most perfect moment of Bob's life.

I can't say. But I can say the next moment definitely wasn't.

The five sticks had been placed in their bases and were waiting for him in the centre of the stage.

Up went the first much-too-heavy plate. Bob spun it, he wiggled the stick . . . and it *worked.*

He did the same with the next one, and the next, until all five plates were up there spinning in unison.

That Vegas crowd, some of whom had just come from a matinee of Penn and Teller and had tickets for David Copperfield that evening, applauded gently. They were old hands. They knew how these shows worked. They understood that the opening moments were a bit of a basic tease, before the spectacle was ramped up.

But it wasn't Bob that ramped it up. It was the sticks.

It was as if they had developed comic timing. They balanced their rotating cargo just long enough to maximise the impact, bending, I promise you, to nearly ninety degrees, before suddenly snapping up and flicking the plates off. The plates were tossed two or three feet through the air, rotating as they went before smashing onto the stage. Quite beautifully the sticks dispensed with the plates one at a time, every few seconds, in a perfect rhythm. After the first plate had gone, you knew exactly what was coming with each of the next four in turn, giving Plate Spinning Bob's show a sense of choreography that it hadn't earned.

As the auditorium watched each stick bow and then dispense with its plate, poor old Bob ran desperately from one to the other, spinning them some more in a futile attempt to rescue the show. The audience gasped before falling into complete silence.

A silence only broken as the remaining plates hit the ground.

From rapturous applause to a mortified hush in about four minutes.

The mystified audience shuffled off as Bob stood on the stage, crestfallen of course. But he was alright. He *must* have known how it was going to turn out. I'm sure he only did it because he wanted to see Vegas, and aside from the performance, we had a pretty good holiday. We took him out and looked after him. If you separate him from the plate-spinning bit he's an adorable man.

I, a true *Big Breakfast* employee, thought it was the best thing I had ever seen.

From that moment on, Johnny Vaughan was on board and I worked on the show to the very end. Some might say that fact is not unconnected with the very end.

But my memories of working at *The Big Breakfast* weren't always good. I say that – what I mean is that I've got a bad memory. I can't remember the vast majority of what happened, something I reckon can be attributed to getting up at 4 a.m. (often after having been out with the production team the night before) every day for two years. We were all living a strange existence in which the working day was over by around 9.30 a.m.

The sequel to 'Bringing Home the Bacon' was 'Streaky Bacon' (again, name first, content later) in which I asked residents to run down their own street, in front of their own neighbours, in front of their own children, wearing nothing other than a rubber rasher of bacon placed in front of their bollocks and/or (one was a hermaphrodite) vagina.

The prize was their own body weight in bacon, presented by the local mayor, something that always adds a stamp of authority and prestige to any streak.

At the beginning of any of these outside broadcasts, I'd include a review of the mid-range hotel we'd stayed at the night before. I'd always review the tea-and-coffee-making facilities and critique an item from the room service menu: 'Last night I went for the chicken jalfrezi: it was first class.' I only tell you this to give you an idea of the freedom you had on the show to do whatever you felt like.

After a heavy night in Southampton, I vomited across the wall and carpet of my room at the Forte Crest. The next morning, the first thing I said on the programme was 'Johnny, could I just directly address the Forte Crest hotel chambermaid who'll be cleaning my room this morning – good luck.' It was a light moment in what was otherwise an awful morning for both me and that Forte Crest hotel chambermaid.

On a Derbyshire estate, whilst telling the viewers of my plans for that morning's 'Streaky Bacon', we spotted a piece of graffiti on the wall next to me saying 'Lee loves Shazza!' I asked the cameraman to home in on Lee's touching tribute – we abandoned our plans for the day and instead dedicated the morning to a desperate search for either or both of those lovebirds.

After all, questions remained unanswered: Why had Lee been so moved that he felt compelled to spell out his desire on that wall? Were his feelings reciprocated by the mysterious Shazza? Is that how she first learned of Lee's feelings toward her? Were the two of them now together? Maybe they had split up and this was the desperate cry of a broken heart? And how did their story end?

I frantically knocked on door after door, asking if anyone knew the stars of that graffiti. No joy. Just rumours I'd picked up from residents. And most of those I couldn't use: they were either filthy, libellous or often a perfect storm of the two.

With two minutes left on the programme, Johnny

Vaughan and Denise Van Outen crossed over to me simply to say goodbye, but I had 'News! Huge news!' The camera pulled back to reveal 'Sharon! I have found Sharon!' Johnny and Denise reacted like I'd discovered Atlantis. It was a rare thing on a throwaway show like that, a genuinely heart-warming moment. Except that Sharon and Lee had now split up and Lee was in prison for aggravated assault.

I also presided over a game in which we carefully placed a beloved family car in a crusher, which at that point was switched off. The game involved the family, who were sentimentally attached to the vehicle, answering questions to save the car. We devised a format that meant it was all very easy, the family would answer the questions correctly and we'd conclude with an uplifting result in which the car was saved. Mid-feature, we spotted a massive flaw. The quiz wasn't easy at all. But we couldn't stop. Not now. The family lost and we were left with no option but to crush their car. Back at the house, presenter Liza Tarbuck, on air, called the feature 'a disgrace'.

Eventually, after two years on the road, I graduated to the house. But filling Johnny Vaughan's seat was intimidating. I presented for the final year, and when you take over from a big personality who really owned the show, you often find yourself asking 'Do the audience like me?' So I decided to ask the viewers if they liked me in a feature called 'Do You Like Me?' They didn't. The next week I did 'Did You Like Do You Like Me?' They did.

Before I was down at the house myself, I'd always go and see Johnny (who is one of my telly heroes) before the show started and watch him play 'show chicken'. Not only did he not rehearse anything, he didn't leave his dressing room until the opening theme tune had started.

He didn't even like to be briefed on what was in the programme. I watched one morning as producer Mike Cunliffe tried to talk him through the two-hour running order. It was five to seven. Johnny wasn't listening. Mike was getting irritated. And in the final handful of seconds before the show began, Johnny finally capitulated by saying, 'Mike, you can brief me while I have a shit.'

The show's visionary executive producer, Ed Forsdick, died suddenly in the middle of 2011.

At his memorial I read out a series of stories submitted to a Facebook tribute site set up by his eleven-year-old son, Linus. This one is from producer Tom Beck. I've included this because it illustrates the evolution of an idea on the programme, and it's a nice insight into the mind of Ed, the greatest light entertainment producer of his generation, whom we all miss. Tom wrote about 'Mowergate', directing his story straight to Linus.

I'd been a researcher on *The Big Breakfast* for about three months when I was put in charge of an odd gardening item where three Hells Angels would test three cordless lawnmowers in the back garden and choose the best. It was based on the ludicrous premise that gardening was the new rock and roll. It was a weak idea – not your dad's, I hasten to add – but the sort of thing *The Big Breakfast* could make fun of. It didn't go well. All three mowers conked out within ten seconds of starting and Johnny went insane with rage. He stormed over to the audience standing at the garden fence: 'Have you ever seen a worse piece of television in your lives?' (They hadn't.) 'I don't know who's responsible but it's a shambles!' I stood at the edge of the garden in horror, feeling absolutely sick.

The show finished and most of the crew sloped off for breakfast but Johnny and your dad stood in heated conversation by the French windows, obviously talking about the lawnmower item. I decided the only thing to do was own up, so I went over, introduced myself and apologised, explaining that it was my item and therefore my fault. Johnny simply stared at me while your dad said, 'It was an absolute disaster; if Chris Evans were here you'd already be fired.' Then they turned back to their conversation and I went to join the other crew, fully expecting that the morning would end with my sacking.

After breakfast there was always a crew meeting where we would go over the show and talk about the next day. That morning only one topic was up for discussion. That day's editor kicked it off: 'Let's start with that fucking lawnmower shambles. It was unforgivable. Tom Beck, it was your fault – what happened?' Everyone turned to look at me, and at that point your dad stepped in. 'Tom's apologised to me and

Johnny; it's dealt with let's – move on.' I don't think I'd ever been more grateful to anyone.

Of course that wasn't really the end of it: your dad based the whole of the next day's show around 'Mowergate – What Went Wrong?' I was credited as 'The Hapless Researcher' and interviewed by Jonathan Dimbleby with a black cardboard strip across my eyes to disguise my identity.

By the time the programme came to an end, we had completely fallen out with Channel 4. There was an enormous gnome that sat in the *Big Breakfast* garden. To the show's fans, it was something of an iconic symbol. For the final episode the then-editor, Ben Rigden, had the gnome loaded onto a flatbed truck and driven down to the headquarters of Channel 4.

Back at the house we watched as the gnome was dumped on the steps in front of Channel 4, its newly manipulated right hand flicking the place the bird.

The Big Breakfast might be the most fondly remembered programme they haven't bothered to bring back. It's a long time since it's ended and I rarely think about it. But of everything that happened and eveyone I encountered, there is one person who does come to mind. In idle moments, I find myself wondering: what happened to Plate Spinning Bob? And the truth is, I don't know where Plate Spinning Bob is today. But of one thing I am sure – wherever he is, whatever he's doing, he's bound to have forgotten his fucking plates.

Chapter 12

BACK OF THE HEAD!

It was August in London's glittering West End and I was about to learn an important lesson.

That sometimes, meeting people off the telly can be very painful.

Especially if that person off the telly beats you up in a toilet.

I'd just finished up on the radio and walked with a few little pals the two minutes across Leicester Square to the 'work pub'.

Later, police CCTV footage would show my assailant waiting for me outside the radio station Xfm and following me on that journey. Personally, it was the first time I'd ever seen him on television. *He wasn't very good.*

As a side note, Leicester Square has to be one of the world's most disappointing tourist destinations. To excitable, impressionable tourists who've seen it by watching too much E! TV it's all shiny, sparkly premieres, Tom Cruise and Anne Hathaway. To tourists who turn up in person on a wet Tuesday afternoon it's all Chiquitos, cheap-looking nightclubs, a vast Yates Winelodge, an Aberdeen Angus Steakhouse, a Bella Pasta and a Subway. If you're reading this and thinking, 'No Richard, you're quite wrong, Leicester Square is excellent and the addition of M&Ms World only makes it even better,' then you and I must part. I'd appreciate it if you would close this book without kicking up a fuss and be on your way.

Good.

Now they're gone, let me take you back to that balmy August evening. The work pub was the Garrick Arms on Charing Cross Road. It takes its name from the next door Garrick Theatre.

Now, the Garrick Theatre might contest this claim, but in the time I worked nearby, productions never seemed to survive very long. And were frequently, let's say, er, bold choices.

There's an old actor's adage or two about that venerable theatre that I once overheard an earnest, glum-looking Terrance Stamp reciting:

> If on the boards of the Garrick ye tread, within a week your play will be dead.
> If at the Garrick you hope to make your mark, 'tis pity because, within a week, the theatre will be dark.
> If it's the stage of the Garrick you're on, in seven days the producers' money will be gone.

Terence Stamp said none of those things, I made

them up, but every time I walked past that place a new production was beginning.

The gap between a poster saying 'Coming soon' and a poster for the same production saying 'Must end tomorrow' frequently felt like hours.

On the fateful night in question (I'm sounding a bit like a policeman here; if you're a fan of encountering policemen, don't go away) the theatre was showing *Bad Girls: The Musical*. You 'eard me. *Bad Girls*, the singing version.

It wasn't a huge success.

I could almost hear the voice of Terence Stamp wailing another old actor's adage that I'd invented: 'The show must go . . . into liquidation.'

The disappointment seemed to have seeped through the wall and into the neighbouring Garrick Arms pub.

There was an air of melancholy in the Garrick Arms that night. It wasn't particularly run-down, but the sort of pub that had wipe-clean menus with photographs of things like chicken fajita burgers on it. I remember it having A4 signs around the place saying 'Look out, bag thieves about', illustrated with a cartoon snake wrapped around a purse. It also had its very own *Deal or No Deal* fruit machine.[24]

The clientele that night was essentially an unstable cocktail of employees from my nearby radio station,

---

[24] The Garrick Arms pub has since had a major makeover (the specialised *Deal or no Deal* frutie has gone, as well as the grotty menus and A4 signs. Sadly it doesn't even sell chicken fajita burgers either.

disappointed-looking tourists, bag thieves and, on this night, a Sky Sports News reporter without a criminal record. *That* was about to change.

I walked in and ordered six pints of beer (I was with five other people, I've not got a problem), and while they were being poured, I popped to the gents. The toilets at the Garrick Arms are down a short flight of stairs, which means that if someone follows you there (for example, a Sky Sports News reporter with criminal intent), there's every chance that the noise your ribs make when they're being kicked won't be heard.

As I was standing at the urinal, I became suddenly aware of someone right behind me. Closer than standard urinal etiquette dictates. I instinctively turned around to see who it was but I didn't get that far as the first punch came thundering down onto the back of my head. I don't remember the beating well. I crouched down, defensively bringing my arms up to cover my face desperately shouting, 'I'm sorry! For whatever it is I've done to upset you.'

I don't know how long it lasted but when he stopped, he raced out.

It's remarkable what the human brain does in a situation like this. Although I was battered I didn't feel any pain, at least not for an hour or two. I went upstairs and clasping both of my hands to my face told my colleagues, 'I've been beaten up!'

There was a moment's disbelief before they noticed the blood on my shirt. I lowered my hands to reveal a boxer's face and a nose that had shifted its spot on my face for the first time in thirty years.

Now this is obviously a bit of a weird situation to find yourself in, so I tried to crack a joke. 'Yeah, but I'll tell you what my main concern is! My concern is whether or not you can get blood out of Paul Smith jeans!' I was surprised they didn't react favorably – they looked at me puzzled – but it turned it was about the sixth time I'd said it: as soon as I got to the end of it my injured brain would forget. That's why so many experienced stand-ups refuse to go out and perform if they're suffering from concussion.

The manager quickly pressed the special emergency button behind the bar that immediately summoned the police. Another detail that added to the romance of the Garrick Arms.

Two cops showed up within minutes and I gave them a statement standing next to the *Deal or No Deal* machine, which was emitting Noel Edmonds' voice on a loop.

The cacophony of statements echoing around my rattled head only added to my confusion.

'Did you get a look at your attacker?'

'The banker wants to make you an offer.'

'Did anyone else here see what happened?'

'Let's see what's in box number twelve.'

'Are you having problems with your vision?'

'Oh terrible luck, you've just lost the £250 box.'

I went to UCH A&E with my friend Marc and Capital Radio's travel girl Louise Pepper. There was no traffic on the way, so she didn't have anything to do. Even though it was a Monday evening there was an hour and a half's wait, so we went to the Lords Indian restaurant near Warren Street. They didn't want to let me in as I was covered in blood and had a glassy stare – but they kindly acquiesced and for that I am truly grateful. However, I won't be going back. What kind of place admits people that have clearly been fighting? A real shame, as the food was excellent.

Back at A&E they told me to undress, and it was only then that I realised there was a patchwork of bruises from ankle to shoulder. I had a black eye, a fat lip and the doctor told me I would probably need surgery to realign my nose. I tried another quip: 'But you should have seen the other guy!'

Yes, I know. It's hopeless, especially given that the other guy was unmarked, but I can't tell you how much pleasure it gave me. It is one of those small acts of defiance that is meaningless to anyone else but doesn't half make you feel better. The doctor didn't laugh, but then again as a Central London doctor he'd probably heard it four or five times that night. If you're a doctor and someone does that joke, just laugh a little bit. It sort of helps.

I was interviewed by a journalist from the *Evening Standard* two days later:

When Richard Bacon enters the Century Club on Shaftesbury Avenue, I almost don't recognise him. His face, usually so boyish, is puffed and swollen, particularly beneath the eyes, where two semicircles of purplish-black have rapidly developed over the past few days.

The skin on his cheeks has a yellowish hue and his nose, clearly broken, is twice its normal size. His split lip is healing well, but his mouth still looks exceptionally tender. He points to the bruises all over his body: down the arms, the thighs, on his back, his chest, even the inside of his ankle.

Then a DJ at Heart FM I had a bit of an awkward night's sleep, and as I arrived at work the next morning, the big boss Steve Orchard took me to one side. It turned out that prior to this job, which seemed to involve a lot of sacking people, he'd been a social worker and counselled trauma sufferers. He's a sweet guy, Steve, and he said, 'I can tell you this much, Rich, whoever did this to you will be listening to your show today. They'll want to know how you react.'

Another listener. I hope Steve appreciated the lengths I'd gone to to grow the audience.

What he told me made me *determined* to make light of what had happened on air. I thought it was a way of letting that guy know that whatever his dopey plan had been, whatever he was hoping to achieve by attacking me in a toilet, he'd failed.

In the opening link of the show I told the listeners what had happened and ironically demanded that every single one of them 'account for your movements at ten past seven last night', so that I could 'eliminate you from my inquiries.'

We put a photo of my battered face online, which generated thousands of hits within minutes. It was touching to know just how many people in London wanted to see me beaten up.

Now, if you *do* ever find yourself beaten up in a grotty pub toilet in the early evening by a reporter from Sky Sports News (who'd travelled for over an hour on a train to do so), there's one golden rule.

Don't make jokes about it on the radio.

Because your thoughtful big boss Steve Orchard will have been correct. Your assailant *will* be listening, and any flippant remarks you make on air could end up being used against you in court.

Charing Cross Police Station is a place I find hard to warm to (in fairness, it probably wasn't designed to look inviting. Top marks to the architect). Within a single month I visited it both as a victim of assault and as a suspect for perverting the course of justice and potentially derailing a murder trial (see Chapter Twenty-One).

This time I went with my brand-new girlfriend because the only person I could think of who'd want to beat me up, apart from some crazy listener, was her ex-boyfriend, a Sky Sports News reporter. You might be able to see where this is going. If you can't, you're a bit slow.

But that scenario *seemed* unlikely. She's so lovely and her old fella had no history of violence.

She was shown the CCTV footage from the Garrick Arms and she gasped as she *instantly* recognised the man on the screen. It was Noel Edmonds. The camera was trained on the fruit machine. However, just a few moments later she spotted something that *really* upset her. 'Oh my god! What's a chicken fajita burger?'

'Not yet, love,' said the officer. 'There, do you recognise either of *these* gentlemen?'

It turned out that *two* men had been involved in the attack: her Sky Sports News ex and his best mate, who came as back-up and guarded the toilet door. The quality of the CCTV footage was poor (when is it anything else?) and she could only formally identify the best pal. But it was enough of a connection for the Sky Sports News reporter to be arrested.

He confessed. He was charged. And a court date was set. All seemed to be on track.

Now, here is where, in all honesty, you could learn a thing or two from my experience. Should you become the victim of an assault, at *this* point – when the police tell you someone's been charged – your reaction will be that it's more or less a done deal. That's how it felt to me. You don't know what the punishment will be, but you already feel a sense of justice.

Well don't. Because at that moment you probably won't have taken into account the murky nether world that exists between defence lawyers and Britain's Crown Prosecution Service.

Because even when handed a mass of good evidence by the police, the CPS will sometimes strike a deal (known as a 'basis of plea') with the defendant's lawyer.

Think of it as bartering. But instead of bartering over,

say, the price of some tracksuit trousers on a market stall, they're bartering over what actually happened. Over facts.

And from the victim's side of things, it can feel pretty outrageous. So in my case, the defendant's lawyer called the Crown Prosecutor and had a conversation that I have never been privy to, but I imagine it went something like this:

Lawyer: Hello Crown Prosecutor, my client is happy to admit that he hit Richard Bacon in that toilet – but he's going to say that Richard hit him first. That OK? Once we've established that it was Richard who hit him in the first place, my gracious client will admit that in hitting Richard back, he probably went a bit too far in defending himself. But all in all, it's clear Richard Bacon is mainly to blame. Alright?

CPS: Sounds good to me.

You might wonder why something like this would happen. As far as I can tell, the CPS do it because they are busy and life is easier if the defendant doesn't contest the charge.

The defendant's lawyer does it because although his client is admitting to the charge (in this case 'Common Assault'), he's managed to water it down.

So, when I say I hope *you* can learn something, I mean simply that if you are a victim of some sort of crime, *doggedly* ask the CPS if they've struck a 'basis of plea'. And if they say yes, *demand* to see it in writing before it is read out in a public court. It's your right. I'd never heard of a basis of plea, so I *didn't* ask about one, and to make matters worse, the Crown Prosecutor on the phone to me two days before the hearing told me they would be presenting the case as the unprovoked attack it was and for good measure explained it was so straightforward that 'there's really *no need* for you to come to court'.

I'm just saying, watch out for this kind of thing.

Having been told not to come to court you can imagine my surprise when reporters began calling me after the hearing asking me about the uncontested claim that I walked into a toilet and smacked a guy.

I managed to get most of the reporters not to run anything through some useful contacts, but that deal, cobbled together by the CPS, the details of that bartered and fabricated story had the potential to seriously damage me and my career. The people involved should have realised this.

I spent months trying to get the CPS to explain themselves. They spent months trying very hard to fob me off. I ended up writing to the Director of Public Prosecutions, and they eventually instituted a review headed by the Chief Crown Prosecutor of Lancashire, a decent seeming chap who had a proper look at it all. He wrote me a letter marked 'Private and Confidential'. Now, I'm sorry decent-seeming Chief Crown Prosecutor of Lancashire, but I don't consider my irritation at the handling of the <u>public</u> court proceedings as either private or confidential.

He wrote: 'I have concluded that the (CPS's) decision to accept the basis of plea put forward by Mr [Sky sports reporter] cannot be justified.'

The letter went on to apologise for the 'handling of case', as well as for causing me 'distress', and concluded by saying that the CPS hoped that 'lessons are learned' from this case and 'any repetition avoided.'

Apparently it is incredibly rare to get the CPS to admit that they cannot justify a decision that they have made. Namely, and to put it in layman's terms, that the CPS should not have let the defense simply change key facts, including their damaging claim that I struck the first blow. I didn't. As the CPS letter accepted after the Chief Crown Prosecutor had reviewed the evidence, it would have been a bit difficult for me to get that first blow in, or any blow, when I had my back to my attacker and never even got to see who he was.

It's all a few years ago now and when I received the letter I decided not to take things any further, I didn't want to waste any more time wallowing in this silly saga. And despite my assailant's attitude towards me, I didn't particularly want him to lose his job.

But the next time you find yourself in the Garrick Arms, and you pop down to use the mens toilet, then I'd appreciate it if you could cast your mind back to what I've written in this chapter. Not for the details about me – for the warning about the bag thieves. Because by the time you get back to your Chicken Fajita Burger, your bag could well be long gone.[25]

---

[25] Just remembered that the Garrick Arms has had a delightful makeover, placing your bag in markedly less danger. The chicken fajita burger has now been replaced with the much posher sounding Mexican chicken flatbread. Oh don't think I can see through your flimsy disguise Mexican chicken flatbread – you're just a chicken fajita burger under a different name.

Chapter 13

HOW I ESCAPED STEWART LEE'S CERTAIN FATE: THE DEATH AND DEATH OF A STAND-UP COMEDIAN

Stewart Lee brought out the definitive book on comedy by a British stand-up comedian called *How I Escaped My Certain Fate: The Life and Deaths of a Stand-Up Comedian*. If you like stand-up, particularly his, I would urge you to read it.

Much of the book is made up of annotated transcripts from three of his full-length shows, revealing the 'inner mechanism' of his jokes. I will now use this technique on my own stand-up comedy.

Here is the annotated transcript of my one stand-up show, performed just once at the Edinburgh Festival of

2009, where I was supported by Reg D. Hunter. [26]

The performance I gave, according to many of the people who saw it or heard it broadcast live on BBC Radio 5 Live, was 'awful', 'dire' and 'a failure'.

Well, three years later, I can finally set the record straight and demonstrate that not only were those people wrong, but that my act was actually funny.

Because the routine was broadcast on the radio and streamed onto the BBC website, I have gone back and studied it. It may look terrible in this transcript, but, for reasons I'll explain, it was actually funny. That's right. Funny. What's written beneath really is word for word what I said. But it's imperative that you read the footnotes as you come across them.[27]

RICHARD BACON'S FINAL FAREWELL TOUR[28]

A transcript of the show recorded on 27 August 2009 at the Udderbelly, Edinburgh[29]

Hello Edinburgh! Hello, thank you![30]

---

[26] Reg D. Hunter had just done an hour and I went on after him for thirteen minutes, so technically that's true. In the course of my one-gig stand-up career, I have only ever been a headliner. It's also worth pointing out that even Reg hadn't had a good time with that audience. There were about 700 of them, it was 11 p.m., they were drunk and restless and had been in their seats for over an hour.

[27] Good. You're getting the hang of it.

[28] I thought this title was gently amusing because I had never performed stand-up before. It would also be funny in retrospect if I performed stand-up again. But I haven't and I won't.

[29] When I came out on stage, I raised my hand in what, I now realise, watching it back, looked like a gesture of triumph. This would turn out to be terribly misjudged.

[30] My producer at BBC 5 Live, Louise Birt, suggested it might be 'fun' if I performed a five-minute stand-up comedy set at the Edinburgh Festival, which could be broadcast live on

What a nice reception. Well, you know, this is my first stand-up routine, it's my debut, obviously I'm a bit nervous. I'm excited as well: we are all now live on the radio. Yes! That's it! Ha ha ha![31]

Erm, so listen, I thought I would start by getting my past out of the way.[32] Let's just deal with this head-on. In 1997, I was sacked from the children's television programme *Blue Peter*.[33]

(MILD CHEER FROM AUDIENCE.)

Don't, don't just . . . so long as you're just cheering the programme *Blue Peter*, that's fine. I'm assuming – just nod – I'm assuming that everyone here knows why I was sacked. Just nod. Right . . . no? No? No? Ooh, someone else? No? Habitual lateness.[34]

Habitual lateness. Man, they're tight on that show.[35] I

---

my radio show. Initially I wondered whether I could write five minutes of comedy. In the event I rambled on for thirteen minutes. The question of whether I can write five minutes of stand-up comedy remains unanswered. But I failed to spot the flaw in this concept. The live set came in the *middle* of my three-hour radio show. In the middle. They built a make-shift studio in one of the corners of the bar outside the venue. I had all manner of guests to get through beforehand; there was just no breathing space. I had to talk and talk right up until I went on stage. I had no time to gather my thoughts. You feel me?

[31] Twelve seconds in, and no jokes as yet. Too long, Richard, too long.

[32] Even though I'd over-rehearsed this act (you wouldn't believe how many times I went through it before the radio programme started that day), for some unknown reason, I actually forgot to do my opening joke. I was going to start with this: 'As we're live on national radio, I'm not allowed to swear, make jokes about politics, or God, or alcohol. It's a bit like doing an open mic spot for the Taliban.' This would have got a bit of a laugh, and had I had a confident start it might have meant the rest of the act could have gone very differently. Hindsight's 20/20.

[33] Now thirty-six seconds in, still no jokes. In retrospect, missing out that original opening was a disaster.

[34] First scripted joke but I *massively* over-delivered the punch line.

[35] Due to a mixture of nerves and the encouragement of a light ripple of laughter, I've now started shouting.

just showed up twenty minutes late to bath the dog, and I'm out on my ear.[36]

(A MAN SHOUTS SOMETHING GARBLED.)

Erm . . . thank you, I didn't quite hear what he said.[37] And I think that might be for the best.

Look, that's obviously not true. I was sacked because I did something bad and was exposed in a Sunday newspaper for having a wild night out and was sacked with immediate effect.

And I should have been sacked. What I did was wrong. I'm not proud of what I did: it was a bad thing.[38]

Ha ha! Someone just said 'What did you do?' You know full well what I did.[39]

But let me . . . look, look . . . uh . . .[40]

(THE   AUDIENCE   LAUGH   AT   SOMETHING

---

[36] When I stop shouting to think what I've got to say next, I become aware the room has gone very quiet. Worryingly quiet.

[37] I did not have any pre-prepared heckle put-downs. This response was entirely off-the-cuff.

[38] What I was hinting at here was that I had taken cocaine, but due to the performance being broadcast on BBC 5 Live, I had been told I was not allowed to mention having taken cocaine, which most of the audience would have been aware had happened. If there were any members of the audience who didn't know I'd taken cocaine, God only knows what they were imagining I'd done. It was so open-ended and vague, they might have assumed I'd accidentally caused someone's death, or punched a woman. I was also required not to celebrate the use of drugs, even in jest, and hence this long condemnation of their use in a five-minute comedy routine. These constraints were probably the most insurmountable flaw of this entire process.

[39] If I'd have said 'cocaine', it would have diffused the hecklers, but the BBC wouldn't allow me to. As a result, the nerves are back and I'm shouting again.

[40] On stage, this is the moment where you can clearly see me starting to wilt. The nerves begin to get on top of me, and my mind starts to go blank. I'd spent too long learning the routine word by word, and now it's getting away from me. If I'd gone in for a conversational style of performance, I might not have started floundering. But because I knew I'd missed the odd word, I panicked.

ANOTHER AUDIENCE MEMBER SAYS.)

No, look, people, this is 5 Live, not Talksport. Please. Um . . . So yes, look, you know why I was sacked, and I was sacked, but here's the thing, hang on, give me a sec.[41]

I am the only person who can tell you what it's like to be sacked from *Blue Peter*, and do you know the strangest thing about losing your job on that programme?[42] They take you into a room and they tell you your contract has been terminated and then they make you hand in your *Blue Peter* badge.[43]

They make you hand in your badge![44]

Yeah, like Mel Gibson in *Lethal Weapon*. But like Mel Gibson, I know the pain of losing that badge.

One minute, by flashing that *Blue Peter* badge, I could get in free to a wide range of adequately good tourist attractions right across Britain. And the next, I was an ordinary citizen. An ordinary citizen, just like you . . . and you . . . like you . . . and you. No, not you, not that ordinary.[45]

---

[41] I'm trying to get control of the room, but I sound like a supply teacher who's not got the confidence to control a rowdy class. The audience can sense this.

[42] We're just over two minutes in, and the audience are suddenly listening very intently. It's impossible to know whether they're really intrigued or are starting to zone out.

[43] This line gets a decent laugh. Great. Everything seems to be settling down.

[44] The adrenaline from the laugh makes me start shouting again. The shouted repetition of this line, which just two seconds earlier the audience had liked, now gets absolutely nothing.

[45] Here I attempt to do a bit of audience interaction, bringing them into the show by pointing at them, and then making a humorous remark about the last one I pointed at. It went down like a lead balloon apart from with the audience member who I claimed was 'too ordinary', who smiled weakly. I am now starting to feel like I'm suffocating. It feels as if the walls are starting to close in, and I'm panicking even more every time I don't say the exact words that I'd over-rehearsed. Things are starting to spiral.

And all of a sudden, just like you, I would have to pay to get into the Motor Museum at Beaulieu.[46] In the extremely unlikely event that I ever wanted to get into the Motor Museum at Beaulieu.[47]

But I mentioned this, and I'm going to move on from *Blue Peter*, but I have to deal with it because it, it, it follows me around wherever I go . . . I'm in the paper today, it mentions it a couple of times, that I'm doing this first kind of stand-up set, and the newspaper articles mention *Blue Peter*, and it follows me around for ever.[48] And it doesn't matter what I go on to do from here with the rest of my life and the rest of my career. However big, however unlikely . . . bring peace to the Middle East. Cure cancer. Invent the teleporter. When I die, in the obit in the newspaper, where you get, you get . . . you have my name, you have that one sentence explanation of who you are, it'll say 'Richard Bacon, the only person ever to be sacked from *Blue Peter*. Oh. And he invented the teleporter.'[49] Um . . .

---

[46] We're three minutes seventeen seconds in and, looking back over the transcript, there's been a maximum of five jokes. That works out as an intentional humorous observation every thirty-nine seconds. That doesn't sound much more than you'd expect in an ordinary conversation.

[47] I've now lost confidence in everything I'm saying and I'm rattling through the set-ups and punch lines in a desperate attempt to move things on. I have started to look down at the floor and am holding the mic stand in a death grip, as if it's the only solid object in a room that's spinning wildly.

[48] Again, this seems like more detail than the audience needs to know.

[49] I'd used this joke once before during a televised interview with Piers Morgan on ITV1, and it went down brilliantly. It was the last line I said after a long face-to-face interview, and it brought the house down, really topped the entire show. Lightning didn't strike twice (but hopefully it did strike again, because you've already read it at the end of Chapter One. Only you know).

But *Blue Peter* isn't the only telly show I've presented. I've got quite a canon of work. I'm going to read out to you some of the other television shows I have presented. Here we . . . you're laughing already.

Here they are. *Rent Free. Get Staffed.* Ha . . . I did a show called *Get Staffed. The Big Idea. Castaway Exposed. Flipside. Back to Reality. 19 Keys.* It's like a parlour game in which you have to list TV shows you've never heard of. Ha. Aha ha.[50]

But, do you know what? I learned a valuable lesson from those shows as well, and that is that it's perfectly possible to lose television gigs without doing anything illegal.[51]

I'm from Mansfield in Nottinghamshire . . . anyone heard of Mansfield? Yes! Someone appeared to boo Mansfield. Er, I love Mansfield, I'm from Mansfield, I'm the third most famous person from Mansfield. This list goes like this – it goes Rebecca Adlington, Alvin Stardust and then me. And you know when you're the third most famous person from Mansfield that you're a minor celebrity. You're definitely a minor celebrity.[52]

---

[50] Suddenly there's a proper laugh from the audience. Watching the video on YouTube, one man in the front row dips his head into his chest, he's enjoying it so much. This is a good line, and one I thought was so good when the best man at my wedding first delivered it, I squirrelled it away, word for word, for future use. The laugh at my wedding was bigger, but then again the audience at my wedding wasn't full of strangers secretly hoping to see me fall flat on my arse.

[51] Another laugh and things look as if they're stabilising. They seem to enjoy me poking fun at my TV career, but I'm acutely aware now that there's absolutely nothing else on this topic coming up. The audience will find that out soon enough.

[52] Nothing from the audience here. I think they might have expected a joke about Rebecca Adlington or Alvin Stardust but, if they did, they didn't get one. Actually, I did have a Rebecca Adlington one, but I cut it out because I didn't want to be perceived as kicking

I think number four on the list, if memory serves, is the fourth most famous person from Mansfield, is Dan Whitehead, who runs Dan Whitehead's Sofa Workshop in Mansfield and he pays for his own TV ads on local television. I mean, right now he has more screen-time than I do.[53]

Soon he'll be number three. Alvin Stardust will have to look over his shoulder a little bit.[54]

But, I, and it's hard, it can be hard being a minor celebrity.[55] This is a true story. I was in Leicester Square, I was in Leicester Square the other day[56] and there's a family there and the father clocked me, and he . . . he . . .

Nottingham on the radio. It was: 'Rebecca Adlington is the real hero of Nottinghamshire, winning those medals at the Olympics last year. Sensational achievement. She's not the first person from round there to get her hands on some gold – but she is the first person from Nottingham to do so without first driving a Ford Escort through a jewellery shop window.' You know. Not bad.)

[53] Dan Whitehead is not the owner of Dan Whitehead's Sofa Workshop. This Dan Whitehead does not exist. The real Dan Whitehead is actually a producer I worked with at *The Big Breakfast* and who was my sidekick when I first started doing Xfm. For a reason I just can't put my finger on, I really like using his name in things. I've told interviewers that growing up, I was inspired by the Central TV show *I'm Dan Whitehead*; I've written scripts where the lead character is called 'Dan Whitehead'; and I briefly considered calling a company 'Dan Whitehead Ltd'. Anyway, all this meant nothing to the audience, none of whom cared for either Dan Whitehead the fictional sofa man from Mansfield, nor Dan Whitehead the TV producer from . . . actually, I've no idea where Dan Whitehead's from. Swindon? Not sure.

[54] This is very Mansfield-specific. Some might say *too* Mansfield-specific. In Mansfield, this stuff would have killed. Being from Mansfield, Alvin Stardust is mentioned probably more in Mansfield than anywhere else in the country – thus, people are just more aware of him. In retrospect, it must have been strange for an Edinburgh audience to hear the name Alvin Stardust out of nowhere for the first time in years, and then no real joke off the back of it.

[55] Some of the audience are thinking 'No, it's not, it's not hard at all,' but this was supposed to be tongue-in-cheek. That said, the audience are still unconvinced about my ability to make jokes, so I think they take this statement at face value.

[56] This is a true story, but my repetition of 'Leicester Square' makes it immediately seem like it's not. It sounds as if I'm about to launch into a hackneyed music hall joke, as I've used exactly the same speech patterns as old-time comics saying, 'Take my mother-in-law . . . please, *my mother-in-law* . . .'

he looked at me and he smiled and he gestured towards his camera. And he said 'Hey, photo?' And I said 'Yeah, sure. Yeah, of course. Of course.' So I put my arms around his daughters, he had two young daughters, I went round like that, and put my arms round and smiled, and he said 'What you doing?' I said 'Well, I'm posing with your . . .' 'I want you to take the photo.'[57]

It was, it was a silly little misunderstanding, you know, we, we shook hands, we smiled, I made some phone calls later and then I had him beaten up.[58]

Erm, but I spent . . . growing up I spent more time in Nottingham. So Mansfield's in Nottinghamshire, and I spent more of my adult life and I worked in Nottingham.[59]

---

[57] This gets a laugh, but afterwards, a fellow comic informed me it was a hoary old chestnut of an anecdote, which he'd heard people say loads of times before. Well, it genuinely happened to me, as described, and it got a laugh, so sue me.

[58] This reads brilliantly on the page, but it just sounded weird in the room. All in the delivery.

[59] I had a huge section here, to bridge between mentioning Nottingham and introducing the Tales of Robin Hood exhibition, which I completely forgot. Here it is: 'Nottingham's a great city. A lot of recent coverage focuses on its gun crime but, of course, it's most famous for Robin Hood. These days, if someone held you up in the city centre with just a bow and arrow, you'd be pleasantly surprised. 'Oh, how quaint! I might survive this.' For years there was an attraction in the centre called The Tales of Robin Hood. It's shut down recently – largely because it wasn't very good, but for years tourists kept turning up and handing over their money. It was actually like a metaphor for Robin Hood. It took from the relatively rich, and gave them something poor. Don't get me wrong – I'm a huge fan of Nottingham. I think there are parallels between Nottingham and the great city of Jerusalem. Seriously, there are some striking similarities. They both have a tourist industry built almost entirely around one person, from centuries ago, who did good deeds for the poor . . . and who didn't actually exist. Hey, look, I'm not trying to be needlessly controversial – I don't believe in him myself, but I can see that there are some people in the room who do believe. I didn't mean to offend any sections of the audience. But you know what – whether or not he actually existed and did the things we're told he did isn't important – the important thing is the lessons he's left behind. Such as, don't get on the wrong side of the Sheriff of Nottingham and, if you're having a stick fight on a log, don't do it against Little John.' Oh, I remembered the Alvin Stardust bit which had no gags in it word for word, but the really big, quite decent

And . . . Nottingham city centre had this tourist attraction called The Tales of Robin Hood, and for a long time I was obsessed with The Tales of Robin Hood. And it shut down just two weeks ago. Just two weeks ago.

And Tales of Robin Hood had this little train that took you around the tourist attraction, and it took you past little waxworks of Maid Marion and then you went through the Major Oak, and it shut down a few weeks ago because it was rubbish.[60]

It was a terrible tourist attraction. And this fact will give you a measure of just how bad The Tales of Robin Hood was. This is absolutely true.[61] That little train that took the tourists around The Tales of Robin Hood was bought second-hand from an abattoir.

It was bought from an abattoir.

So the train that took the tourists around, in a previous life had taken the animals on their final journey to the kill-room,[62] and after that had transported their dead carcasses from kill-room to cold storage, and that was the

---

(you know-ish) chunk of cleverly written stuff? Fell by the bloody wayside.

[60] It's coming together now. I've relaxed a bit, although I'm going too fast, but I'm getting a lot of information across, the audience are listening, and suddenly it looks as if things are turning around. Could be a big ending. Just so long as I don't get heckled by someone who says something funny and steals my thunder. Not long to go now.

[61] I know it's a cliché and you don't trust stand-ups when they say this, but this *is* entirely true. Let me state the fact once more: the train that took the tourists round The Tales of Robin Hood in Nottingham City Centre was bought second-hand from an abattoir. Even though I can't see or hear you, I can tell you're laughing. See? *Funny*.

[62] I invented the term 'kill-room' for this act, and have since used it once or twice in casual conversation as if it were real. No one has ever questioned me about it when I use it, and the audience all seem to accept it without concern. If the place where they kill animals in an abattoir is genuinely now called a 'kill-room', then I would like to make it clear that I invented this word in 2009. It would be lovely to think that this routine had some sort of legacy.

same train. And I went to The Tales of Robin Hood and I sat in that train and, in some ways, I envied those animals.

I envied those animals because they will have experienced a number of heightened emotions as they went on that final journey on that train to the kill-room, to their death. A number of heightened emotions. But none of them will have been extreme boredom.

FEMALE HECKLER: Are we ALL on that train now?[63] Erm, I . . . er, no, uh hur ha ha.

LIGHT APPLAUSE FROM THE AUDIENCE.

Yesterday I was trying to think of the ultimate definition of being middle-class.[64] What is that ultimate definition, and I've come up with it. This is it. You are definitely middle-class when you have that conversation about what starter you'd do on *Come Dine With Me*.[65]

Ha ha haa. Erm, goat's cheese is such a cop-out.[66]

---

[63] I remember once hearing David Baddiel say that the biggest lie in stand-up comedy is that heckles are funny. He reckoned that there had been, at best, two funny heckles in the history of comedy, and the rest were all just witless yells from drunken idiots. Annoyingly, in my debut gig being broadcast on national radio, a heckler shouted out with something which was funny, dismissive and witty. Half of me absolutely wilted, the other half was genuinely amused. If David Baddiel is reading, I would appreciate it if he could update his hypothesis regarding heckles to incorporate the world's third funny example. I have since told the story of the heckle so many times, it's now one of my better anecdotes, and watching the actual event back on YouTube, it was a bit of a let-down compared to how I've built it up. It ends with a fictionalised coda, where I say 'Right, before I go, just two things . . .' and someone shouts out 'Make it one' which, when I watched the video back, didn't happen on the night. After the event, I built the gig up in my mind into a humiliating defeat of massive proportions, with a hilarious and mocking audience outdoing me at every turn.

[64] Christ, this bit comes out of nowhere. Clunk.

[65] The observation gets nothing. The audience have been too jolted by my sudden leap from one topic to an entirely different one. Still, there's always the line which tops it to come.

[66] Nope, it's dead in the water. Time to bail.

Er, listen, thank you very much, it's been very nice to speak to you all, you've been lovely. Thank you, you've been on the radio. Thank you.

That was a terrifying experience but I got through it,[67] thank you for staying.

I've been Richard Bacon, you've been Reg D. Hunter's audience. Goodnight![68]

---

[67] I make the mistake here of self-reviewing, which makes it sound as though I've done well. I haven't.

[68] Bit of a Ben Elton catchphrase sign-off, there. I'm so excited to finish that waves of relief hit me as I start the farewell and I get much too fulsome considering the reception I've received. Audience members on the front row started rushing out as early as I say 'Er, listen . . .' The following day, *The Guardian* gave me a lukewarm review, which I will boil down out of context: 'Good'; 'A nice line in self-deprecation'; 'not exactly topical'; 'proved less rewarding'; 'by the end had gone off the boil'. They summed up by saying, 'A comic once told me that there's only one thing more difficult than your first stand-up gig. Your second stand-up gig.' To be frank, I couldn't care less. That's never, *ever* something I'm going to do. Still, the radio show was one of the best ones I've ever done – it going badly, and then me being slated by guests and callers for the next two hours was awesome. A lot of people told me the show had 'Sony Award' written all over it – and it did. Only it turned out the words 'Not ever nominated for a' preceded them.

Chapter 14

HALF HOPPING LIKE A HUNCHBACK

Everything about this story is grotty.

Its conclusion, its participants and most certainly its setting.

Our tale begins in late 1996 in no particular sports bar. It doesn't matter where particularly (mainly for legal reasons. In fact, it is not 'no particular sports bar', it's a very particular sports bar, a particularly horrible one, but the lawyer says I can't tell you which one it is lest my publisher end up in a legal fight with the bar, which the publisher might lose because, I would imagine, this sports bars has seen a lot of fights).

Put simply, this must be one of the worst places on the planet. But Richard, I can hear you saying, while I have no doubt in your ability to judge the quality of any given bar – I know you go to lots of them – your view might be out of date. Perhaps the years have been kind to this particular sports bar.

Dear reader, you raise a most understandable concern. And I don't want my soliciting of your opinion to be a purely cosmetic exercise. So I have listened to your view. And I have acted. To write this chapter, I have returned to this particular sports bar.

It is a Wednesday night early in the brand-new year. I have checked their website for opening times and now find myself on the opposite side of the road, gazing at its facade. My first thought (well, after 'I can't believe it's still going') is just how utterly unchanged it is. There have been four people call themselves prime minister from the last day I was in there to today. There have been tsunamis, 9/11s, Middle East wars, every single episode of *The West Wing* and ironic teenage magazine show *T4* (cruelly taken from us far too late) and, through it all, this bar has remained exactly as it was.

Age has not wearied this sports bar. Nor the years condemned. It's always been shit. And I imagine it's come close to being condemned.[69]

There are two types of people in the world. People who are willing to give this sports bar a try. And people who have done so once. So accompany me now, as I grip you by the hand and we prepare to take a trip inside this

---

[69] If I had a lawyer, he'd probably like me to stress that this sports bar has never come close to being condemned.

sports bar on a cold February night. (If you're a bloke, we'd better not hold hands, I imagine it won't go down well.)

Look, here it is. And there, by the front door, there's some velvet ropes. What's that you say? The velvet ropes are a bit short and not really fulfilling a function? Look, just be quiet, we don't want any trouble before we've even got in.

That said, there are two things which if you see them outside a bar indicate it's not going to be very nice inside. One is if they have pointless velvet ropes at the door. The other is if they have some fat unfriendly bouncer in a black satin bomber jacket standing behind them, eyeing anyone who approaches suspiciously for no reason, even though the bar is empty. We pass the pointless velvet ropes at the door, and walk past the fat unfriendly bouncer in a black satin bomber jacket standing behind them, eyeing us as we approach suspiciously for no reason, even though the bar is empty.

I know what you're thinking: 'Why is it that the first person you see in this sports bar is someone who's clearly never done sports in his life?'[70] Shhh! He might hear you. And he's probably on drugs.[71]

As we go in, you're pleasantly surprised, as you thought I'd been exaggerating about how horrible it would be and now you know I wasn't.

---

[70] Threatening to do martial arts on a customer is *not* a sport.

[71] To my knowledge no bouncers currently or formerly employed by this sports bar or any of its subsidiaries or associated companies have ever taken illegal drugs. *To my knowledge.*

The first thing you notice is how dingey it is. The ceiling's really low and there are hardly any lights on – it's a bit like entering an aeroplane when the emergency illumination has come on after a fire.

I don't know about you but I don't really like plasma screens in bars, and I'm pleased to say this sports bar doesn't have one. It has ninety. Relax because a few of them are broken.

Those flat-screens are the main source of illumination. They cast the exact same light you'd get if you went round to the house of the old fella who lives on your road who no one's seen since Christmas Eve, and on breaking down the door on a dark, mid-January evening, discover his corpse in a living room, the only light that of *Celebrity Pointless* flickering over his still, cold body.

In a straight choice, between being that dead old man – slumped and rotting in a high-back winged chair, completely alone but for the voice of Richard Osman saying, 'The films of Angelica Houston . . . you could have had *A Cat in Paris*: that would have been a pointless answer,' soon to be buried in an unmarked council grave – or remaining in this particular sports bar for a moment longer: well, you know what it would be. We take a seat by the bar. We can sit anywhere: there are plenty of empty spaces. A Chelsea–Swansea match is playing on the TVs. It is five minutes in. The commentary is so loud, the punters can't hear themselves not think. Without moving my head and just by looking up, I can see nine of those tellies.

But those nine are not only broadcasting an irrelevant Premiership match. Four are showing something else altogether on Eurosport, with the volume turned down. Which means that the format of this particular sports bar – the business proposition – appears to be an attempt to cater for that corner of the market which wants to drink lager out of a jug in front of a football match while keeping an eye on some ski jumping they can't hear.

Oh, I see you've picked up the menu. Careful where you put your hand. It's covered in BBQ sauce. Make sure you don't put it down on the bar, all the crumbs will stick to it. And you're a little perplexed. Don't worry, so am I. I don't want a 'jug' of lager. I don't want a Sex on the Beach. And I certainly don't want a drink called a 'Quack Quack'.

In desperation you turn to the back of the menu (watch that smear of Thousand Island – oops, too late), but there are no more drinks there, only an advert for an upcoming major sports event, which this sports bar is celebrating by doing exactly the same as they usually do, but only if you've booked in advance. The two of us feel unsettled as, periodically, aggressive football chanting breaks out.

Every single table smells of wind.

I find it a sensory war on five fronts. I can't see much. I don't want to touch anything. I refuse to put the food in my mouth. It smells of men. And all I can hear is distorted football commentary.

If I was in Al Qaeda and they locked me in here for a day, I'd definitely tell Jessica Chastain all about Abbottabad.

While I thought it would be an amusing trip down memory lane, it's turned out to be horrible. And I'm sorry to have dragged you in here with me.

After a while, it just made us both feel nervous. So, from the writing of this sentence on, dear reader, you need to know that I've decamped to the much more enjoyable surroundings of a (fairly) nearby members' bar.

An attractive waitress has just apologised to me because she fears the pianist is playing Elgar's *Variations* a little too loudly. 'Hang on,' you're thinking, 'while that apology nicely illustrates the difference between that particular sports bar and this members' bar, I didn't hear any Elgar.'

Alas, I'm afraid I haven't taken you with me. I've imagined you don't work in the media and thus probably don't have membership to this place and I'm afraid 'muggles' (as we call *all* of you who don't work in the media) can't get in. Sorry, I don't make the rules. But do let me know how that Chelsea–Swansea match turns out![72]

Actually, it's quite nice to have a bit of time on my own – you were becoming a bit of a bore.

And it is *very* different in here. Although the Victorian chandeliers and the tealight candles in vintage glass holders in this bar are technically low lighting, unlike that sports bar, the darkness is not there to conceal a load of aggressive blokes wearing tracksuit tops and baseball caps. Almost nobody here has the name of their child written on their back in Olde English script.

---

[72] Don't.

The last thing I saw as I hurried out of that sports bar, apart from the petrified look on your face as I abandoned you, was a man roughly my own age leaning against the bar. He looked every one of his thirty-five-odd years. He wore crumpled trousers, a mournful face and no wedding ring (it was unlikely he'd hidden it as there were no women in there at the time).

I looked at that man with revulsion. Not because I didn't like him – but because he took me back to a different time. Like him, I too one night, single, hopeful, stood at that selfsame sports bar. I too was an unmarried man. And like him, I was a loser.

So this is a cautionary tale and one, I hope, that we can all learn quite a lot from.

In my early twenties, I used to hang around with a man whom I considered to be my best friend. He would eventually go on to betray me, as you'll now know. Let's call him Jack (I can't remember if I identify him in that earlier chapter and can't be bothered to check).

Jack and I were single, young and out on the town. One Friday night in 1996, we found ourselves inside the belly of the beast – this particular sports bar.

Jack and I got chatting to a girl called Claire. She was hot. Really hot. She was smart. She was sexy and cool. And she was entirely out of place in this sports bar.

The friend she was with, Amy,[73] was an idiot. She was entirely in of place in this sports bar.

---

[73] For obvious reasons I have changed Amy's name. I think I have anyway, I can't actually remember what her name was, so I may have hit upon it by chance.

Amy was stumbling around all over the shop, sweating, shouting and being rude. Occasionally she was doing that thing where someone who's really drunk suddenly goes quiet and you think they might be sick. She was so drunk that at one point she genuinely believed that this sports bar was 'alright!'

I tried to pair off Jack and Amy-the-Idiot, but he wasn't having any of it. He buggered off home, I stayed. Claire and I were getting on great. We just clicked. And because she was driving that night, she was totally sober. If someone flirts with you when they're drunk, it means nothing. But if they flirt with you when they're sober, in legal terms, it means things are more likely to happen.[74]

Even in the nightmarish surroundings of this sports bar I could see that Claire was absolutely lovely. Porcelain skin. Smart. Well-dressed. Fun. How could such a delicate flower have blossomed in the arid surrounds of this sports bar? Actually it wasn't that arid, there was a puddle of Foster's, vomit and sweat on the floor. Thanks, Amy.

But as I looked around, I could see hungry eyes in the darkness, eager to pluck my precious bloom. The potential suitors came in every imaginable variety: from what looked like 1970s football hooligans to violent-looking 1980s-style football thugs; from men with spider's webs tattooed onto their faces to men with spider's webs tattooed onto their necks. All human life was there.

---

[74] Just to be clear, in legal terms, it means nothing.

I made it my mission to rescue Claire from these hellish surroundings. I didn't want her to get entangled in another suitor's web (those tattooed prats have confused the metaphor). And my intentions were entirely pure: I wanted to spend the night with her.

She leaned over and gently, coquettishly whispered, 'Would you like to come back to my flat?' But I couldn't make out a word of what she said because the Tartan Army next to us were shouting, 'The referee's a wanker!'

'What did you say?'

'Do you want to come back to my flat?!' she repeated.

'Is it in this sports bar?' I asked.

'No, of course it isn't.'

'Then yes.'

But there was a hitch. Claire added, 'But I've got to drop Amy off on the way.' As a gentleman, I didn't complain that this was eating into my sex time, but instead agreed with the plan. Both girls lived in flats somewhere not far away. I squeezed myself into the back of Claire's two-seater sports car. She owned a sports car. This was getting better and better.

And then it stopped getting better and started getting worse.

The only safe thing to drink in this sports bar, unless you like shots that are on fire, or Quack Quacks (which may or may not be on fire; I've never ordered one) is pints of lager. I'd had quite a lot of them. The amount of liquid, the heat of the car, the motion, even my own boyish excitement all acted upon my body and I quickly found myself gagging for the lavatory.

You know when you need to go to the toilet so badly that you can't concentrate on what someone is saying? Imagine then being folded into the back seat of a sports car, so small that even Ryanair's Michael O'Leary would refuse to sell that seat, or at the very least wouldn't consider charging a disabled person extra to use it.

Add to that the fact that in lower-end, road-hugging sports cars, you feel every bump, hole and divot of the road, and I was like a tin of Coke being shaken up.

The situation became so acute I couldn't speak. I was so uncomfortable, I half expected Corporal Lynndie England to wander over with an unlit cigarette in her mouth and pose for a photograph with me.

When we pulled up outside Amy's place, I had only one option.

'Amy, can I use your bog?'

My voice came out much higher than normal.

Claire said, 'We're only two minutes away from *my* house.'

'I know, I'm sorry, but I really need to go *now*.'

This was an awful moment. The chances of sex had, I knew full well at that point, somewhat dimmed. But I believed they had not been extinguished. A flicker of doubt had flashed across Claire's classically beautiful face, but in the light of the car that came on when the door opened, I could still see *some* desire behind that convulsion of mild disgust.

My long-held dream of having a one-night stand with

a girl I had met in a ropy sports bar was still intact.

Claire had to let me out of the back by getting out of the car and folding her seat forward, which somehow made things even more undignified.

Amy told Claire she might as well come up too. Amy's flat was on the second floor. We trudged (I half hopped like a hunchback) into her front room. Even today, sixteen years later, so great was my relief that I can recall exactly the precise layout of annoying Amy's flat. I could draw you a floor plan. A corridor extended from the back of the centre of the living room. First on the right was the kitchen. Next to it, a bedroom. Directly opposite was the toilet and, at the end of the corridor, the master bedroom.

I left the girls chatting in the living room and darted for the lav.

I bolted the door and looked around this impossibly small bathroom, tore off my belt and clasped myself to the toilet seat.

Now, if Jane Austen had ever written about such a scene, this is the moment she'd ask you, the dear reader, to allow her the dignity of drawing a veil over the details of what happened in that tiny facility. Suffice it to say, Jane, it was an all-guns-blazing unpleasant few seconds.

As soon as it was over I stayed rooted to the seat. Enveloped by the calm that followed the storm.

Outside, I could hear Amy talking to Claire. She was hammered and so was bellowing very loudly. They were talking about nothing in particular. And suddenly she said something that chilled me to the marrow: 'You've not been here before have you, Claire? Let me show you round.'

Oh Jesus Christ, no.

I reached for the canister of air freshener on the window sill and pulled the trigger. It was empty.

I heard them getting closer. 'This is the kitchen. Nice in here, isn't it? All this stuff was here when I bought it.'

I turned to the window but it wouldn't budge. I pushed again and again in desperation. It had been painted shut.

All I could do was slip out, open the door just a tiny amount to slide out and leave behind my shame. There was every chance that a tiny toilet wouldn't be on the tour's itinerary. Everyone knows what a tiny toilet looks like. They would probably skip past straight to the master bedroom

I went and stood in the living room. And waited (it was pre-Twitter, so I had nothing to do).

Suddenly I heard Amy saying, 'So, this is the guest bedroom.' My heart soared, the logical progression from guest bedroom is to go to the main bedroom. Isn't it? Anyway, I held my breath. Unfortunately I was the only one doing so. There was a pause and I could hear a door being opened.

'And this . . .'

Amy stopped. The next thing I heard was her screaming, '*He's had a shit in my flat!!!*'

I do hope Jane Austen stopped reading before this point.

But as Jane would understand, there is simply no way

of recovering from a girl you fancy having the words 'He's had a shit in my flat' wailed into her face.

Claire, being nice, and sober, didn't comment. The two of them came back into the living room. Neither spoke. I pretended I hadn't heard a thing, which we all knew was impossible considering I was a maximum of twenty feet away from them at any point in that flat. Both were staring directly at me though, the way you might look at someone you'd caught daubing graffiti onto a war memorial.

The awful silence was only broken when Idiot Amy started laughing at me, which was worse than the silence.

As Amy's braying laughter echoed through my head, I realised my long-held dream of having a one-night stand with a girl I'd met in a ropy sports bar had died.

Claire gave me a lift to her flat. We said nothing on the way to each other, until we parked and she suggested I get a cab home.

In the days, months and years that followed (I couldn't stop hearing that damning sentence about my legitimate use of the bathroom at the property of another, echoing through history) and as the years passed, I became increasingly angry.

Claire, I would now like to address you personally.

How *dare* someone who went to this (for legal reasons unnamed) sports bar and was clearly willing to sleep with a man she had just met look down on him for doing something that *everyone we admire* – like Gandhi, Princess Diana and Mother Teresa — did as a routine matter of course. How dare you, Claire?

What I did was entirely natural. But your behaviour was appalling. You *should* have had sex with me that night. The fact you didn't reflects very badly on you. Very badly.

But I'm the better person. Claire, I am willing to let bygones be bygones, provided you admit in writing that your behaviour that night was *dreadful*.

If you can do that small thing, then we can put this whole sorry mess behind us and meet up again in that sports bar, this Thursday at 8 p.m. Oh and Claire – *this time* I'll have been to the toilet first.

Chapter 15

SUPERMODEL ELLE LIBERACHI BEGS ME FOR SEX: THE TRUE STORY

In 2010 I was either the subject of a *News of the World* sting, a Mossad honeytrap or, at the very least, I had inadvertently come into contact with an incredibly attractive woman who would do anything to have sex with me.

Elle Liberachi sent me seven photos[75] attached to an email dropped into my inbox from nowhere, while my wife and I were having a low-level argument about whether BBC2's *Miranda* is any good. Bear in mind, this was 2010. (We all know now it is, but back then the nation had yet to make up its mind. I told her it was.)

Hey mr,

Been such a long time hun, how are you? Lost all my

---

[75] Google image her. See? Yeah, you knows it.

contacts when my laptop crashed when i was NY last week, sucks big time! But i got your email from Liz, its been such a good year so far, so many big campaigns.

Finished filming the movie, was only out in LA for a month as i was walking for NY fashion week, but it was all good, just couldnt wait to get home!!!

If you make it out to SA, let me know i will give you the details i was staying at the most amazing place! away from everything, a real chilled out atmosphere.

Hit me back on here, Facebook, mobile or this email is the way forward, dont be a stranger.

Elle x

Now, what would *you* do? Seriously, what would you do? Obviously I'm married, I've been the subject of a scandal in the past and I didn't want to go the way of Jason Manford. Then I looked at the photographs again. And I knew I had to act.

The first thing to do was try and work out if this was an email from a supermodel who wanted to have sex with me, Mossad or the *News of the World*.

Hey mr, [a bit impersonal but friendly]

Been such a long time hun, [yes, it's been thirty-five years and we've still not actually met]. how are you? [confused and slightly aroused.] Lost all my contacts when my laptop crashed when i was NY last week [no, this is sounding more like a sting], sucks big time [ooh, she's young and said something that could be construed sexually, and which I've chosen to take that way]. But i got your email from Liz [hmm, common enough name, could be a sting again], its been such a good year so far, so many big campaigns [I'm lovin' this model talk].

Finished filming the movie [I shouldn't imagine that'll be getting a theatrical release], was only out in LA for a month as i was walking for NY fashion week [ooh, more model jargon], but it was all good, just couldnt wait to get home!!! [I think overuse of the exclamation mark is the worst punctuation sin – but in a potential affairee, it is by no means a deal-breaker].

If you make it out to SA [South Africa, no time difference, can be done in a weekend – all good], let me know i will give you the details i was staying at the most amazing place! away from everything, a real chilled out atmosphere [the spectre of the sting is back again, things just sound too perfect].

Hit me back on here, Facebook, mobile or this email is the way forward, dont be a stranger [all of these forms of communication leave a paper trail, and I certainly wouldn't be a stranger to anyone if I appeared in the *News of the World* a few weeks later embroiled in a sex scandal].

Elle x [possibly not Elle, but a middle-aged investigative journalist with his fingers crossed]

Having weighed up the evidence, I decided that it was at least *feasible*, just feasible, that it was in fact the supermodel/sex option. Elle and I had, I reckoned, at least an outside chance of a brief and illicit future.

Matters, however, took a turn for the worse when my wife Rebecca caught me emailing her back. Rebecca, not one to get wound up very often, was genuinely annoyed with me when she saw the email I'd written.

And yet all I'd said was, 'Elle, please send me a photo where your breasts are exposed.'

No, of course I didn't. I said, 'Elle, please send me a photo where your vagina is exposed.'

No, of course I didn't.

All it said. ALL IT SAID was 'Thanks.' That's it. Thanks. Just a single word. Nothing suggestive. Zilch sexual. Simply and solely 'Thanks.' Well, Rebecca acted as if I'd sent the vagina one.

'What's wrong with being polite?' I demanded to know. After all, this woman, whom I've never met before, had very kindly sent me seven pictures of herself in a bikini. The least I can do is say thanks. If someone made an effort to send you something nice, I told her, you'd thank them. We all would. Even more so if that gesture came from a stranger. A lovely young stranger.

Rebecca told me that by replying *at all* I was tentatively opening up a dialogue. An exchange of any sort, a reply, turned it into a conversation and that it was from these tiny green shoots that full-blown marriage-wrecking moments blossom.

'Don't be so silly,' I told her. Yes, it was the beginning of a chat, but that's because I thought we could be friends with Elle. She looked very sweet. Perhaps we'd all get on and go to the cinema together.

How nice it would be to have a new friend. And that was why I was dipping my toes in the water of a possible two-way exchange. And perhaps hoping that water might book me a ticket to New York or South Africa for illicit sex.

Irrespective of Rebecca's anger, the more I thought about it, the more I started to panic. What if it was a Mossad honeytrap? Suppose the Israeli secret service had discovered I had hosted *Young Voters' Question Time* on BBC3 (better than it sounds) and wanted to blackmail me so that I would stop asking even-handed questions about Palestine? Oh God. I'll end up like Mordechai Vanunu, sitting in solitary for eleven years.

By the time I'm freed, Elle will have lost all her appeal, she'd be at least thirty-one, and undoubtedly they'll have given my daily 5 Live show to someone else. Probably Colin Murray. Too much is at stake. I can't take the risk. I must walk away.

Almost as soon as my mind was made up, my phone buzzed. Elle had enclosed another photo along with just a single sentence email. 'Richard, do you have Skype?'

Right, that's it! The game's up! Come out, come out wherever you are, grubby little reporter! Trying to secure footage, no doubt, of me saying something mucky to a beautiful, large-breasted blonde. We've lost *too many* good TV presenters that way and I am damned if I'm going to be just another statistic. Sorry guys. Better luck next time.

P.S. If I got the wrong end of the stick entirely and it wasn't a newspaper sting . . . And you're not working for the Israeli secret service . . . And you're deffo gonna keep things quiet . . . And you're not mental . . . Then Elle, I would be more than happy to have sex with you. The only thing I must demand from you is total secrecy. I'm sure you understand. And if it helps swing the deal, I've just ordered the Skype.

Some months later, after I'd spoken publicly about receiving this strange email, Elle Liberachi's agent got in touch with me and wanted it made clear that Elle had not intended to contact me and that she did not, to the best of her agent's knowledge, want to take me to New York and/or South Africa. She said that if I was to ever publicly speak about this again, I should make this clear.

I accept this and so am including that little detail in this book. It is, of course, only fair.

Her agent sounded very annoyed at the time, but I would point out that an agent is never privy to everything their client does, says or emails. Perhaps, for reasons of her own, Elle didn't want her agent to know she was fixated with me. I'm not saying this happened, but I think we should all (and that includes you, Elle's agent) keep an open mind about this and not just jump to hasty conclusions regarding what Elle does and doesn't want to do.

Elle – ball's in your court.

Chapter 16

FLEE, THAT'S THE MAGIC NUMBERS

The Guildford Four.

The Birmingham Six.

The Wood Lane One.

They are just three examples of a major injustice. For the Birmingham Six and the Guildford Four, the truth is now known. Their nightmare is over. But not for the Wood Lane One.

Wood Lane was the address of Top of the Pops in its latter years. And the one? Well, that's me. And this is the tale of how the misuse and misinterpretation of a single adjective can lead to a very silly mess.

Because it's all about language and I didn't want to make the same mistake twice so I've brought in a guest author Charles Dickens. This is quite a coup, he hasn't written anything since abandoning his novel *The Mystery of Edwin Drood*. He has come out of retirement for this one-off short story.

He says it might seem even more authentic if you read it in the voice of Patrick Stewart.

In the heart of every Englishman must lie a special place reserved for the ramshackle buildings comprising the vast BBC TV Centre. Any Briton who discovers himself standing before the looming facade, towering over Wood Lane like a vast glass headstone, will find his mind cast back to childhood, a miasma of felt-hewn Muppets, tin-plated Cybermen and Mr Kenneth Everett's unnatural performance as the strumpet Cupid Stunt.

At every hour of the day, fat-cheeked producers scuttle past, their absurd haircuts and paper cups of coffee bobbing as they do, making their way to the bowels of the building, where their daily toil consists of constructing the finest televisual jewels in the whole of the Empire. And 'The Royal Bodyguard'.

Can any man look at such an institution and not feel the irresistible surge of patriot pride coursing through his breast? Is this not a place of dreams and triumphs? Could any man find himself in such a place and not bear the creep of a smile pulling the edges of his mouth into the broadest of grins?

Perhaps one such gentle man. Let us look at him now.

Watch the way he wanders, saucily, as if he knew no such thing as misfortune. Everywhere he looks, agog, with eyes hungry for new sights on which to set his butterfly gaze. But like any human animal constructed of muscle, bone and tissue, he was unable to see what was still to come.

As he made his hustle and bustle past the security detail, how much futurity did our young hero see?

Did he foresee himself shortly upsetting four of the musical world's most celebrated groupings? Could he have comprehended – nay, even dared dream! – what lay around the corner of time? Namely, a most apoplectic pair of shaggy-bearded minstrels and two delightful, apple-cheeked young backing maidens, copiously weeping tears of heartbreak. Richard Bacon did not.

Aye, Richard Bacon, for that was this chap's name – one that he had borne since leaving his hometown in deepest Nottinghamshire to seek his fortune in London town.

That day (a day, it would transpire, which was soon to become a world of sorrow and trouble), young Bacon was due to present a moving-electric-book show (as I am Charles Dickens, I do not know what a television show is and this is the way I might describe one) entitled *Top of the Pops* live on BBC1. By his side would be the delicate, doll-featured, sweet-natured vision of gentle femininity known to all as Fearne Cotton. Before the transmission they met in a little room to make their introductions (it was the make-up room, but that is not important to our little story).

At the dress rehearsal, the exhibition of the evening's musical turns had passed without remark. All agreed that Richard and Fearne's utterances had been as flawless as a diamond in a maharajah's turban, and all was met with the most generous appreciation of the assembled crowd of teenagers and the unemployed.

And now we come to the critical moment of Richard's fate.

Enter the Magic Numbers.

Briefly perusing the mechanical autocue, Richard absorbed its details: a 'link', in the parlance of the tele-visual industry, which made much mention of the band's familial ties and sweet, melodious harmonies. It ventured to state that they had been forged, as 'twere, in a 'big melting pot of talent'.

Old wives will have you believe much – not least that 'there is many a slip 'twixt cup and lip', and there is much to commend these old maids' hard-won wisdom!

Flushed with excitement from the success of the portion of the show that had just passed, Richard made the error for which he would later be feted on Channel 4 News (I do not know what this is, but let us proceed). He added just a word – a single word, a mere syllable, but three letters long – and proceeded to give voice to his welcome.

Now read on, as Richard Bacon takes up the story.

Thank you, Charles. And sorry readers, that didn't really work out as I'd hoped. He doesn't half go on a bit.

You could sum up the whole thing so far as: 'I presented an episode of *Top of the Pops* with Fearne Cotton and had to introduce the Magic Numbers with a scripted line about their family-based talent.' I regret exhuming him now.

Before I tell you any more about the story, let me make one thing clear to you: I never meant to say the word 'fat' in relation to the band themselves. That is something I wouldn't do, and it's something I didn't do. But I can understand why the band thought I had. They did nothing wrong, and I did nothing wrong, they believed I *had* done something wrong, but I *hadn't* actually done anything wrong, but I can sort of see why they thought it. Got that? Good. Let's continue.

I was supposed to introduce the Magic Numbers on to the Top of the Pops stage with this scripted link: 'What do you get when you put two brothers and two sisters in a band? A big melting pot of talent. Go wild for . . . the Magic Numbers!' Like most telly folk, I don't read autocues word for word – adding a word here, dropping a word there, trying to make it sound more casual, more genuine. And so instead of saying, 'a big melting pot of talent', I elongated it a bit and said, 'a big fat melting pot of talent'.

So in fairness to the Numbers, the word 'fat' wasn't on the autocue, and in fairness to me, they're two words that just naturally go together, like 'strawberry' and 'shortcake', or 'Leveson' and 'Inquiry.' I meant 'big fat' in the way it was used to describe that person's Greek wedding in the film. I meant it in the way it was later used in the titles *My Big Fat Gypsy Wedding* or *The Big Fat Quiz of the Year*.

The Magic Numbers were a band I liked and was

playing on my Xfm show. I didn't want to give them a generic intro. I wanted to make it stand out. I wanted them to enjoy it. Well, stand out it did. Enjoy it they did not.

Within seconds of uttering those words, Cotters began gesticulating passionately and shaking her head. I did not understand what she was trying to convey. Had something gone right or had something gone wrong?

The band played their track 'Love Me Like You', and left the stage.

I noticed some of the crew whispering. Minutes later, the executive producer, Andi Peters (yes, that one), came to tell me that not only were the band unhappy, not only were the girls 'in tears', but they were refusing to come out for the show.

This, he told me, was a disaster for a live show due on BBC1, in prime time, in half an hour.

And all of this was happening, he added, because I had called them fat.

I told Andi Peters that:

(a) I hadn't called them fat (well, I'd said it, but not in that way, and that

(b) I would go and smooth things over with their tour manager or whatever member of their record label was hanging about.

Unless you, in the flesh, have been backstage and seen a popular band, almost any band, about to do a live set on telly when they've got a single in the charts, you'll have no idea just how many people come along for the ride. You might only have a dude with a guitar, but he'll turn up with twelve people from the label (they have perplexingly similar titles like Head of Artist Liason, or Head of Artist PR Liason, or Artist Liason to the Head of PR), and they often come across less like a group of work colleagues and more like a slightly frosty, good-looking cult. If you ever walked into a classroom at school which was filled with all the cool kids, you'll know what it's like – you open the door of the room they're in, they stare back underwhelmed; you smile, they half look away as if you're insignificant; you leave and as the door shuts, you hear them all laughing.

I told Andi I had no doubt that their rep would totally understand what I'd done. That he'd see that rather than insulting the physicality of his act, I had simply complimented the familial origins of this talented combo and with added adjective. I assured Andi my charm would work.

I was led to a member of their team. Certainly not a member of the band, but somebody who did something (as you now know there's lots of somebodies who do somethings around bands). I took along the *Top of the Pops* floor manager for support. I began the explanation using as warm a tone as I could muster but the somebody-who-does-something wouldn't even make eye contact with me. I can't have been more than two sentences through it when he cut in impatiently and angrily with: 'Calling my band fat is the equivalent of you introducing a band who happened to be black as a bunch of niggers.'

Wow. Gosh. I mean, really, what do you say to that?

The answer is nothing. You don't say anything because at that point you know you're talking to a mad person.

I walked away flabbergasted. And a bit confused.

Rather than returning to Andi Peters as I had anticipated, flushed with the success of clearing up the mess, I was returning to Andi Peters having been accused of fatism *and* hypothetical racism.

I tried to speak to the band members personally, to apologise for the crossed wires that, to be fair, I had caused, but was told in no uncertain terms that I was not allowed anywhere near them.

A few minutes later, and just twenty minutes before transmission, I watched as the band climbed into a black people carrier, a black people carrier that the somebody-who-does-something probably thought I'd insult if I ever had to introduce it on telly, and fled.

They were replaced on the live show by a video of Goldfrapp.

On Channel 4 News, Jon Snow announced, 'Shamed *Blue Peter* presenter Richard Bacon strikes again.'

Two months later, the *NME* published their Fool List to find 'the most offensive, irritating and generally fucking useless' person in the world. I won. Here's the full Top Ten:

1. Richard Bacon
2. David Cameron

3. Prince Harry

4. The jury who acquitted Michael Jackson

5. The Who

6. George Bush

7. Coca-Cola

8. James Mullord (no idea who he is)

9. Tim Westwood

10. James Blunt

It's worth noting that this list was published immediately after both the start of the Iraq War and the release
of James Blunt's *Back to Bedlam.*

I have since run into the blokes from the Magic
Numbers in the lift at Capital Radio, initially a bit
awkward, I grant you, but we made up.

The Magic Numbers are nothing but good news.

There are still thousands of references to this nonsense
online.

And that got me thinking, well, made me sad to know
that, given *Top of the Pops* has now played its final tune,
and said its last goodbye, I had generated *Top of the
Pops'* final ever negative media storm.*

---

*Apropos of nothing, I wrote this chapter in October 2012.

POSTSCRIPT

Eagle-eyed readers might have noticed that the first half of the chapter was written in the style of Charles Dickens and the second not. This is because the Charles Dickens bit was taking too long and I got bored.

Chapter 17

LAZY, LAZY JOKE

April 1997

In Tatton, Cheshire, a heroic white-suited former BBC war correspondent named Martin Bell is standing as an independent against the sitting MP Neil Hamilton on an anti-sleaze platform. He is about to make history as the first independent MP since before the war.

In western Africa, an outbreak of meningitis devastates the region, creating tens of thousands of orphans; elsewhere the country is being ravaged by Aids.

In a cramped office at the University of London's student union, the entertainments officer Ricky Gervais is planning the next month's programme of events.

Over at BBC Television Centre, a fresh-faced Richard Bacon is about to present only his fifth edition of the long-running children's television programme *Blue Peter*.

And in America, the home DVD player had just been introduced.

No one knew then (or at least, if they did, they didn't speak up) that eight years later, these disparate elements would collide and ruin my life/the second half of an evening.

Corporate awards are an essential part of the canon of any mid-ranking presenter. The trick is to pretend that phrases like this mean something to you,

'So, let's take a look at the nominations for Best Below the Line Campaign.'

For the second year in a row I'd been booked to host the Home Entertainment Weekly (HEW) annual awards (me neither). The previous one had been my first 'corporate' and it had gone well. I'd been rebooked. 'This corporate stuff is easy,' I said to myself. Like taking candy from a load of drunk babies (in ill-fitting suits).

Arriving at the prestigious QE2 conference centre in Central London at 4 p.m. for a rehearsal, the event's producer Steve bounded over and told me he had slipped a joke of his own into the script.

He told me that that heroic, white-suited former BBC war correspondent Martin Bell would be making a surprise appearance to thank the kind people of the Home Entertainment Weekly industry (it sounds more baffling each time you hear it) for donating money to an African charity that he was involved with.

'As Martin Bell leaves the stage,' Steve told me, almost

conspiratorially, 'you come back, look as if you're really welling up because what he's said is so moving, and then say, 'and all of that money will, of course, be given straight to those lazy, lazy African orphans.'

Looking back at it eight years later, I still can't quite comprehend what the joke was supposed to be. If I pull it apart, I think it's a casual way of saying that starving people in Africa are relying on Western charity money because they're too lazy to help themselves out of poverty. If that IS the essence of it it's just unpleasant. Or maybe it was straight-out sarcasm, but even if it is straight-out sarcasm it is the sort of gag that Ricky Gervais, in his most provocative mood, at the height of his powers, at his *own* gig, after he's won the crowd over, might have got away with. And I stress Ricky Gervais *might*.

I, however, was due to talk to a room of pissed people who weren't particularly keen to hear from me. They wanted their award, they wanted to get wrecked on free, low-rent Pinot Grigio and they wanted to have extra-marital sex with Hayley, the new HR assistant. Nothing else.

'Steve, I'm really not sure this'll work,' I said. But my paymaster brushed my concerns aside. 'No, it'll be fine. Just do it. It'll be hilarious.' Steve knew these people. Steve was bound to be right.

The event had been going moderately well. Hayley the new HR assistant had been nominated for a curious number of awards and the award for Best Integrated Marketing Strategy in the North-West was behind us (well done Roger Andrews). The end was in sight. It was time for me to introduce our special guest.

'Ladies and gentlemen, Mr Martin Bell!' As he took to the stage I decided that this would be a wonderful opportunity for a little break. I sidled off stage, whipped out my BlackBerry (this was a few years back), cracked open a cold beer and didn't listen to a word Mr Martin Bell said.

It was explained to me afterwards that he had made an incredibly moving speech. I've now watched it back from a video they recorded of the night. He spoke from first-hand experience of meeting some of the 'beautiful children' trapped in an endless cycle of poverty, famine and disease that would be 'empowered by the generosity' of each and every person there. In what, I can see now, was a heartbreaking eight-minute speech he held the room spellbound as he explained that every pound they'd donated didn't just make a negligible difference, but that those pounds had given some children 'the chance of life'. I also discovered later that this had made a few people cry. As his final words carried across the auditorium he called them 'heroes'. There was a spontaneous standing ovation.

I, meanwhile, was texting my mate Johnny.

Hearing the applause die down, I slipped the phone into my pocket, sauntered back up to the lectern and read word-for-word what was waiting for me on the autocue. Words written by Steve. And Steve wouldn't be wrong. Steve knew his audience.

'And all of that money will, of course, be given straight to those lazy, lazy African orphans.'

At first there was total silence. I imagine some of them, like me, didn't really understand it: that's the sort of silence that means you're in trouble. I tried to carry on – 'Well we come now to the Best Packaging award' – but was cut off by boos. Actual boos. It is a very strange thing being booed off stage. It is intimidating and yet the only reaction that naturally comes to you is to smile. Which makes people boo more.

The only person I knew in the audience overheard the folk on his table (one of whom was the woman who'd booked me) talking about how I 'can't possibly carry on. He HAS to leave now.'

I didn't leave straight away. I tried to plough on. Staring back at me was not just a depressing sea of half-eaten plates of chicken in a creamy tarragon sauce with a trio of vegetables, but three hundred faces riven with contempt.

The last word I heard as I left the venue that night was 'wanker'.

I wanted to say, no, I'm not the wanker. Steve's the wanker. I didn't want to do the bloody joke. I don't even understand it. And anyway, I don't think African orphans are lazy. Well, they might be but I . . . wouldn't know. Because I don't know. I've got nothing against them.

But it was hard to start that conversation with anyone, because none of them would make eye contact with me.

The following year's Home Entertainment Weekly

awards was hosted by Alex Zane. I don't know if Steve asked him to do that gag again, but he was booked for a second year so it's seems unlikely.

Anyway, this has been a long-winded way of saying it is time to make up for this horrible event. I have decided there's only way to put this right – to donate the whole of that night's fee to charity. Not my fee, Steve. Yours. And Steve, I've got some more bad news for you. Every penny of it will be given straight to those lazy, lazy African orphans.

Chapter 18

SQUALID SEX UNDER A TABLE

When you think of me, what do you think of?

My excellent broadcasting on television and radio, of course.

My smooth, rich voice, once used for a long-running Blockbuster video campaign, until they replaced me with the actor Christian Slater – I doubt they'll be using Christian Slater again, unless he becomes a corporate administrator.

The Channel 5 quiz show *19 Keys* ('short-lived' – Wikipedia; 'not particularly competent technically' – UKGameshows.com).

But regardless of what you think, there's one thing you probably don't associate with me.

Two people having squalid sex under a table.

Well, that's about to change.

Let me take you back to the happiest day of my life. (I should probably make it clear at the outset, I'm not one of the people having squalid sex under a table. I've never had squalid sex under a table.

It was my wedding day and everything had gone perfectly. The venue was exquisite, the flowers beautiful, the service a heart-warming affair. (I'm using the word 'affair' there to mean 'event' rather than 'squalid romantic encounter'. Although I will be using it later in the other sense.)

As I sat on the raised dais, between my new bride and my old mother, I could not imagine anything able to spoil what had been a flawless day.

And then two people had squalid sex under a table.

As I sit back now, nearly five years later, I cannot help but wonder at which point during the moving ceremony two of my guests, previously unknown to each other, gazed into one another's eyes and decided they would end up having squalid sex under a table.

Perhaps it was during the speech by the father of the bride, or the serving of the delicious macaroni cheese side dish, or the spectacular reveal of the disco in an adjoining room – which they didn't attend, as the dancing clashed with their schedule of having squalid sex under a table.

Regardless of what moment it was, one thing is certain: two people ended up having squalid sex under a table.

At a stroke (don't say 'or more than one stroke, Richy mate', I dislike all manner of innuendo[76]), my wedding

---

[76] Don't mutter 'in-your-end-o' either, it's utterly moronic.

had gone from being a high-class affair to something you'd expect from a high-class escort. (I say 'high-class' because the repetition sounds good, but in truth, a high-class escort would not have squalid sex under a table. That would be something a regular escort would do. The high-class one would probably only use the table to eat an expensive meal off, before having squalid sex with a fat married businessman in an expensive hotel room.[77])

I will not accord them the dignity of identifying this squalid couple by name. After all, there's every chance they had no idea of each other's names while they were having squalid sex under that table.

But I believe there is an unspoken agreement regarding weddings and it is this: none of the guests will engage in sexual intercourse before the bride and groom have been afforded the chance. Well, that was not a courtesy extended to me and my wife on our special day. If we'd known what was to happen, we'd have put gravel under all the tables and placed a bucket of cold water on every centrepiece. That or brought our own sex forward by a number of hours.

Now, whenever Rebecca and I look back at the photos of that delightful day at Somerset's Babington House, I do not see Rebecca's radiant smile. I do not see my father's proud, beaming face. I do not conjure up scenes of our friends toasting our future with affection and love.

---

[77] I'd actually booked some expensive hotel rooms on site, which meant the high-class escort option *was* open to them, but they decided to opt instead for the regular escort package. Unbelievable.

All I can summon in my mind's eye is an image of an old colleague drunkenly rutting under a table with a woman he'd said a maximum of thirty words to in his life.

The wedding gift they gave us turned out to be an unpleasant image. And unlike most of my wedding gifts, it's one I have been unable to return.

Chapter 19

JESUS. BUT BETTER

Sometime around AD 25 in Galilee, a bearded man without a job turned up to a wedding in Cana.

Rudely, he made an immediate beeline for the bar because, like a lot of bearded men without jobs, he was intensely interested in free alcohol.

Due to some terrible planning on behalf of the bride and groom, all the wine had run out. I don't know who this dopey couple were, but that basic misunderstanding of how to treat guests at a wedding doesn't, in my view, make them deserving of a world-class miracle.

Halfway through the best man's speech, which without anything for the guests to drink must have seemed like it was going on for twice as long as normal, the bearded man couldn't take it anymore.

According to a chap called John who wrote an eye-witness account (although we now know those eyes didn't witness it and he wrote the story a hundred years later), the bearded man's mum was there. So not only was he denied a drink, his mum's presence probably meant he wasn't allowed to smoke. As John recounts, she leaned over to him and said, 'They have no wine!' To which he replied, 'O Woman, what have I to do with you?'

Nagged by a high-maintenance mother; listening, I'm guessing, based on other best man speeches I've heard, to a badly delivered joke lifted from the Internet; unable to enjoy a fag and with nothing on the table to slake his thirst, the man suddenly took matters into his own hands.

He used His magic to turn all the water . . . into wine.

That man, as you've no doubt already worked out, was Jesus.

The Bible doesn't specifically say which type of wine He created. If it was Echo Falls or Blossom Hill, I suspect the guests would have preferred it if he'd just left it as water.

But if we boil that story down, Jesus' miracle was turning up to someone's nuptials and spiking the punch.

If you're one of the millions of people who divine the view of the Almighty from bizarre episodes in the Bible like that, then you have to divine that this tale demonstrates – unequivocally *proves* – that God endorses getting half-crocked at weddings.

I am not, as a point of principle, against God's stance. Everyone's entitled to their opinion. But even the most devout worshipper could hardly call God's (and by proxy Jesus') attitude to drinking at functions socially responsible.

Which is why this chapter is dedicated to demonstrating why I am more socially responsible than Jesus.[78]

Some moons ago I was in a relationship with a clever and beautiful young lady who, for religious reasons, didn't drink alcohol. She also wasn't that keen on me drinking alcohol – understandable, there's nothing worse than being sober when I'm drunk. She was also aware that me and alcohol at that period of my life somewhat diminished my trustworthiness. So she asked me if I wouldn't mind giving up.

Being a nice sort of chap, I said yes.

But being a not very nice sort of chap, I didn't mean a word of it.

The problem is I'm not a very good liar.[79]

So I'd come home from a night out, reeking of grog and a last-minute frenzied consumption of Altoid breath mints, and she'd say, perfectly reasonably, 'You've been drinking.'

I would say, 'No, I haven't.'

And she would say, 'Yes. You have.'

'Young lady,' I would counter, becoming unnecessarily

---

[78] If you think that's a bit controversial, let me quickly put your mind at rest. I'm not saying I'm *better* than Jesus but when it comes to being responsible, then, yes, I am better than him. Although we share much in common, I too have been at many weddings where my mum's aggressively tried to get access to yet more white wine but, unlike Jesus, I did not facilitate her being giving more. In fact, on occasion, I've actually lied to my mum and told her the venue's run out of wine solely so she has to move on to water. Usually she's had so much wine by this stage that she doesn't even question this unlikely sounding scenario, or notice the constant stream of bottles of white wine being delivered to the surrounding tables.

[79] Some of you might say the problem is not so much that I'm a poor liar but more that I lied in the first place. Oh, because *you're* so perfect, aren't you? You're a hypocrite. You make me sick.

grand, 'No-no, I did not. I ate some trifle, and as everybody knows, trifle has loads of sherry in it.'

'It looks like you've had about six pints of that trifle.'

'Well . . . young lady,' (now just buying time, and repeatedly pointing at nothing with an outstretched finger) 'that trifle had *a lot* of whatever spirit they put in the trifle . . . in it.'

I was vague about the specific spirit in the trifle because I've got no idea whether trifle has any alcohol in it. I can't stand trifle.

Quite reasonably, the next morning she decided that my duplicitous trifle behaviour would be met with consequences.

Serious consequences.

She asked me to remove *all alcohol* from the house.

Effectively a ban.

Prohibition had come to One Percival Mews in Chiswick, West London (One Percival Mews was the modern mews house I lived in for five years. I refer you back to Chapter Six).

I was not going to take this sitting down but because I was so hungover I couldn't get up, so I did.

There was a concession, however. She agreed that *one* bottle of Chateaux Something-or-other (I've done a generic name there; it's not actually some cheapo brand you might get in Aldi) could be kept in a small cupboard beneath the hobs for when my dad came to visit.

That cupboard, in effect, became my own speakeasy.

But not some sexy speakeasy bar with huge mirrors,

black countertops and a clientele of showgirls and sharply dressed gangsters, but a speakeasy decorated with one of those big bottles of olive oil with chilies in it, a mug tree and a George Foreman Grill.

Just like in Bugsy Malone, if you pressed the front of that cupboard, the entire contents would flip over. But that's because it was flimsily constructed.

One evening, while my girlfriend was away working, I brought my friend Marc back to the house.

We'd had a few but wanted more – and what could be better than tasting the sweetest nectar of all . . . *contraband*.

The following morning I came down to the kitchen to find that empty bottle of naughty wine staring right back at me from the middle of my peninsula unit. [80]

I didn't have time to go out and buy a replacement. But I knew my girlfriend would get home before me and that she would check that cupboard. She did that for a good reason, because she knew that I couldn't be trusted, so she would *always* check that cupboard.

To you this might seem like a terrible fix: the bottle's empty, it can't be replaced and so the drinking of the wine will *surely* be discovered. But, my friend, you are not a master booze criminal like I am. I knew at once what to do: I filled the bottle up with water, squeezed the cork back into place, trimmed the foil around the lip, wiped

---

[80] A kitchen island unit that's connected to a wall. Yes, *of course* I would rather have had a full kitchen island unit, but the house was not just ugly, it was really badly designed.

it down and stuck it back next to that George Foreman Grill, the chilli oil and the mug tree.

'Flawed!' you're thinking. 'Idiotic!' 'As crap as your trifle lie!' Oh, my friend, I pity thee in thy naivety. The dark-green glass on the wine bottle meant that the liquid inside could barely be seen. The weight was right, you could see movement inside but the colour of that liquid was an irrelevance!

It looked totally legit!

Somebody carry me shoulder-high from the room! (Actually don't: modern mews houses in Chiswick have impractically low ceilings.)

It was the perfect crime and, like all perfect crimes, the deed would never come back to haunt me in any way whatsoever.

THREE MONTHS LATER . . .

Tina Hobley is an excellent actress on the BBC television serial *Holby City*.

For a reason I don't entirely recall, I'd been running a slightly bizarre weekly feature about Tina Hobley on Xfm called 'How's Tina Hobley?'

My colleague Dan Whitehead would impersonate her on the telephone and we'd have a chat about nothing. The feature was just cartoon-like nonsense but if you were Tina Hobley and you heard it you be totally confused as to why we were doing it and, not only would it be a bit unsettling, you'd probably assume it was some kind of strange personal attack on you by a man on the radio you'd never met.

Now, it wasn't an attack, it was just radio silliness with an actress chosen at random.

Each week, I spoke to Tina (Dan) live from her (his) home in Bishop's Stortford [81]

An average episode would start something like this . . .

'Good afternoon and how's Tina Hobley?'

'Richard! Richard! I can't see!'

'Tina, open your eyes!'

'Ah, yes, that's better.'

Silliness.

It's worth saying, at this point, that Dan doesn't really do successful impressions. Unlike Mike Yarwood or Alistair McGowan, Dan simply used his own normal voice, and Dan's voice is not a normal one,

So imagine my surprise when, one day, after a chance meeting with her husband, Tina Hobley invited me to dinner.

She knew about this feature and yet had graciously decided to rise above it all. Not only did she invite me to dinner, she invited my girlfriend. This was extremely generous, especially when you consider the only interaction we'd had up to that point was me and Dan presenting a mentally impaired version of her on the radio – a feature the invite made me immediately drop.

And because I'd done this weird feature, I felt nervous

---

[81] I don't think Tina Hobley lived, or ever has lived, in Bishop's Stortford. Just another reason why, if she ever tuned in, she would have found the entire thing absolutely mystifying.

as I headed to her Chelsea flat. I went straight from work (it was a harder day than normal: I'd had to come up with a new feature to replace 'How's Tina Hobley?') but called my girlfriend on the way and asked her to bring the Hobleys a gift.[82]

I arrived before my girlfriend, and Tina's fiancé Ollie greeted me at the door and lead me through their elegant and luxurious apartment to the kitchen, where he proudly showed me the 'pork done four ways', that he'd been preparing – including a slow-cooked belly pork that he'd been gently simmering for forty-eight hours.

Forty-eight hours. So much work. Two entire days – and I'd forgotten to mention that my girlfriend doesn't eat pork.

Ollie and Tina, being gracious, weren't fazed.

My girlfriend arrived and brought two gifts – a tub of Ben & Jerry's and a bottle of wine.

I was given dispensation this night to drink (she was relaxed about drinking anyway on nights like this) and Ollie served us some of the best wine from his cellar: three-hundred-pound-a-throw bottles. I've had less expensive cars.[83]

The evening was great. The hours had disappeared as quickly as the wine. It was nigh on 1 a.m. and none of us wanted it to end, but the fancy plonk had been quaffed.

They had nothing left in the house. 'Ah!' said Ollie,

---

[82] They're actually the Wheelers but it's just confusing to put that in the main bit of the story. You know her as Tina Hobley, so that's what we're sticking with as their family name, but they aren't the Hobleys in real life, they're the Wheelers.

[83] And more expensive cars, obviously.

suddenly springing to his feet. 'There's the wine you two brought!'

He dashed into the kitchen and emerged victorious, clutching the bottle my girlfriend had brought and three empty wine glasses.

I don't think I had ever been happier to see a bottle of wine. From the jaws of defeat sprang forth victory.

But in a matter of moments, victory would crawl back into defeat's gob.

Ollie removed the cork and began to pour.

Where I expected to see red wine, I saw a transparent liquid. In my drunken state, I didn't click. A similarly pissed Ollie didn't notice either. He sat back and raised the glass to his lips. I remember *so clearly* what happened next.

Ollie sipped. Paused. Scrunched up his face. Paused some more. Then shouted, angrily, *'This is water!'*

Do you remember those old train departure boards? The ones with the slats that rotated impossibly quickly, locking into position one after another to spell out the times and destinations of trains? One of those now whirred and clattered in my head.

But instead of saying 'MANCHESTER PICCADILLY . . . (clickaclicka) . . . PLATFORM 16 . . . (clickaclicka) . . . 9.04 . . . (clickaclicka) . . . NOW BOARDING', it spelled out 'MARC . . . (clickaclicka) . . . MY HOUSE . . . (clickaclicka) . . . WINE . . . (clickaclicka) . . . WATER . . . (clickaclicka) . . . THAT GIFT . . . (clickaclicka) . . . SHIT'.

I had to think quickly. Do I come clean and watch as the entire lie unravels in front of my girlfriend? This could lead to an immediate row – and I did not want to angrily discuss personal relationship matters in front of *Holby*'s Ward Sister Chrissy Williams, whom I barely knew.

Or do I take the noble route out and make up a story so that no one starts shouting at me and losing their temper? I decided to go with my gut instinct.

It was a lie that had got me into this situation – it would be a lie that got me back out.

'Really?' I said, trying to sound convincingly shocked. 'Are you sure? Let me try it.'

I cupped the glass and affected swilling it round a few times like Jilly Goolden. I was a bit worried I might be overdoing it but everyone was so confused that no one noticed.

I took a sip.

'Hmm, well, it certainly *tastes* like water.'

But as I placed the glass on their coffee table, I broke down and confessed. I told the whole story from the beginning to the end, and I held my hands up and begged for their forgiveness.

Did I fuck.

And besides, I didn't need to because Ollie immediately rode to my rescue and announced that I 'must have been conned' by an unscrupulous off-licence and that I should march round there the next day and give them hell.

I told him I would and gave him the impression that I could barely contain my anger: 'Grrr, those bloody . . .

those bloody wine *con artists* . . . doing that! . . . You read about this sort of thing happening all the time!' (this is actually the first time anyone has read of that happening) 'but you never think it will happen to you!' (it won't).

In humble surroundings (well, they weren't – the flat was majestic, but I'm trying to make this sound biblical), in front of a gathering of a good-hearted television actress, my kindly ex-girlfriend and a mildly pissed whatever-it-is-Ollie-does, I had performed a better miracle than Jesus.

I had turned wine into water.

If you *are* going to perform one of Jesus' miracles in reverse, it might as well be this one. Making a sighted man blind wouldn't make for a gently amusing anecdote in a book, and neither would feeding five thousand people to two fish.

Think of this as the Parable of the Liar from a Modern Mews House in Chiswick.

The moral is this: If you're going round Tina Hobley from *Holby City*'s place for dinner, just take her some flowers.

Chapter 20

THE WRONG BOX

I don't know, dear readers, if you've ever been pitied by someone half your age, who's been on telly for about ten minutes and works in a tanning salon.

Well I have. It was at a big television awards show and I'd received a personal invitation from the head of ITV. They'd even reserved me a seat in their exclusive box. Oh my God, I felt like royalty.

I opened the door and there before me were the cream of ITV's big names.

Good evening, Chris Tarrant. How's it going, hero David Jason? (Looking these days a bit more like Uncle Albert than Del Boy . . .)

Why, who's that spilling out of a glamorous dress? It's none other than Irish lovely Christine Bleakley. Pass the chipolatas. This is the life.

As I looked for my seat, one of the commissioners rushed over and I extended my hand, ready to clasp his and thank him for letting me dine on chipolatas with the hosts of *Daybreak* (it was just before all that went south). Instead, he took me by the elbow and whispered, 'Sorry, Richard, you're meant to be in the box next door.'

Oh right. Oh bugger. I see. Right.

You see, it turns out ITV had two boxes and I was in the *other* one.

If I call those boxes 'ITV1' and 'ITV2', you get an indication of the sudden drop-off in quality.

As I walked into this secondary box, my own mid-ranking celebrity status, achieved over a long, fifteen-year slog, was underscored by the standard of my fellow invitees.

Chris Tarrant was replaced by Kerry Katona.

David Jason by *The Big Reunion*'s Lisa Scott-Lee.

Holding court in the centre of the box was Kerry Katona, best known for selling seventy-five-piece Tex Mex Iceland platters and king prawn party crowns. And for marrying minicab drivers who then bankrupt her.

I didn't talk to any of these people. Partly because I was taken aback by the fact they actually existed in real life.

The only person I had a conversation with was Amy Childs, then in the first flush of fame from her appearance on the wrongly Bafta'd *The Only Way Is Essex*.

Amy will only be remembered in history for vajazzling. That's a process by which she spells out people's names in diamante stickers on a woman's front bottom.

It is considered a romantic gesture.

That's because there is no deeper declaration of love

than seeing your name written out in fake diamonds nestling between strands of your girlfriend's pubic hair.

If Shakespeare were alive today, he could have saved himself a lot of bother, bypassed those sonnets and gone down a rough nightclub in Stratford-upon-Avon with the name 'Anne Hathaway' spelled out in fake rubies above his cock.

(Although at twelve letters, he's going to be at the vajazzling parlour for quite a while and it would set him back £89.99 plus VAT. I hope she's worth it, Shakey.)

As I munched on a bit of pitta bread (they hadn't paid for hot food in Box Two), Amy looked up from her phone and said to me, 'Ahhhhh' (you'll, have to imagine her now characteristic Essex voice yourself; I can't do it with words) 'I recognise you from somewhere.' I told her that I was Richard Bacon. No response. She then enquired 'What do you do?' I told her I present the afternoon show on BBC Radio 5 Live.

She smiled sweetly and put a heavily manicured hand on my shoulder.

'Ahhhhhhh,' she said again, 'never mind. We've *all* got to start somewhere.'

I was polite to her that evening but now, here in the hallowed pages of this book, let me get one thing straight with you, Amy Childs, formerly of *The Only Way Is Essex*.

I'm not saying I've got the biggest job in the land.

But let me be clear. It's further up the bloody showbiz ladder than sticking plastic jewels to strangers' crotches in a tanning salon.

Listen love, I interviewed the Foreign Secretary the other day. You think he has 'Ffion' etched in his bush? (I don't know if William Hague's baldness is down to alopecia. If it is, I apologise for this offensive remark; if it's not, the observation stands and I will go to my grave with it.)

I can state this with absolute certainty: there's *no way* I'll be bumping into Amy, formerly from *The Only Way Is Essex*, at that awards do next year.

She's been moved up to the ITV1 box. I'll be lucky if I can still get in the ITV4 one.

Chapter 21

FIVE NIGHTS BEFORE CHRISTMAS

I'll never forget that call.

'Twas the icy cold morn of 20 December a few short years ago. I was just settling down to watch a DVD (remember them?) of series one of *Heroes* (remember that?). I'd just broken up for Christmas from my Xfm *Drivetime Show* (I realise you don't remember that). I could barely be in higher spirits.

I was wrapping a few presents at home when the phone rang. My ringtone was set to 'We Wish You A Merry Christmas' (it wasn't, I just want to make this sound as Christmassy as possible. I think ringtones are for the simple).

It's Dan Thompson, the boss of our parent company, a slightly rotund fellow who'd make an excellent Santa Claus (again, not actually true, I refer you to my answer given in the previous bracket).

'Dan! Ho ho ho! Hey, Dan, so . . . what sort of pizza does Good King Wenceslas order when he calls Dominos? Deep pan, crisp and ev—'

'Richard, I've got two Metropolitan Police officers standing in my office. They want to interview you on suspicion of perverting the course of justice.'

'That's not the right answer, Dan.' Dan's never been very good with jokes; when it comes to corporate restructuring, though, he's yer man.

My first thought was that this was completely mad.

Apparently not.

You see, during the previous day's Xfm radio programme I had, as usual, asked the listeners to 'send me in a mundane text'. These mundane texts could be about *anything*.

They may actually be mundane. They may not be. They were just listeners telling us something about themselves, out of nowhere, with no particular context. And within the context of the radio show, they seemed funny. They seem less funny written down on the page, I must say, so you'll just have to go with me on the funniness bit.

This was one of the first to pop onto my studio text screen that day:

> Dear Richard, I'm serving on a jury so I can't really say anything. Alan.

Now, that sort of text was exactly the type that I

wanted to be presented with on Xfm. There's an element of danger about it. There's a court case. It's ongoing.

Just mentioning it would make the station manager jump.

That's if he was listening. Which he probably wasn't. He was more likely to have been listening to Dan telling him, 'I know you've only been here fourteen minutes, but we've just decided upon a bit of a restructuring, and unfortunately . . .'

I knew at once that this text would allow me to skate close to the edge of one of the cardinal laws in broadcasting. That you have to be *incredibly* sensitive when discussing an active trial.

In meeting after meeting this rule had been drilled into us: don't say anything that could influence a jury. Nothing. Ever. You won't only get sacked, you might end up in prison, they told us.

I thought that I could skip up to the parameter of what was allowed, dance on the boundary, and pull back.

The listeners were canny. They knew what I was doing. So I broke the rule. But I broke it ironically. The key word in that sentence is 'ironically'. For the police the key words in that sentence are 'broke the rule'.

'Oh texter Alan,' I said, 'come come, tell me *all about* that trial, give me the details and I will tell you whether to go *guilty* or *not guilty*. And in exchange you can have a free 'My Chemical Romance CD.' There was a theatrical pause before I added, 'One man's liberty will turn on how much you like emo.'

A running gag on the show was about how much Xfm's listeners had turned against My Chemical Romance for being melodramatic, and American.

Now, little did I know that on this day I had a new listener – *an officer of the law* (always more fun to say or think that phrase to the rhythm of that moment in Rod Hull and Emu's *Pink Windmill*: 'There's somebody at the door! There's somebody at the door!')

This serving copper it should be stressed, did eventually turn up at the door, and with a colleague. And this serving copper was also an entirely *new* addition to the usual Xfm listenership – in that he had a job, had had a haircut in the last three months, and the nearest cannabis to him was locked safely away inside an evidence room rather than behind the cardboard back of a Sanyo hi-fi system in his bedroom at his mum's house.[84] (Although he too probably dreamed of meeting Pete Doherty – not so they could jam together, so he could get his force's arrest rate up.)

This officer immediately reported my on-air comments to his superiors.

When I arrived at big boss Dan's office in our Leicester Square HQ, the first thing he told me was that the police had left.

Yes! It's over! Christmas is back on track! 'Hey, Danny, what's Santa Claus' wife called? Mary Chris—'

---

[84] If anyone from Xfm (the second most enjoyable place I've ever worked after *The Big Breakfast*), is reading this and is thinking 'That's a bit unfair, Richard, to characterise all of our listeners that way', then I would say only this: go to a listener's house and look behind the cardboard back of his Sanyo hi-fi system in his bedroom at his mum's house.

'Richard, they have indeed left . . .' (Again, Dan, wrong answer.) I knew this damn thing would disappear as quickly as it had arrived; that something with so little foundation had even got this far was ridiculous. 'They have left because they listened back to the broadcast and decided the offence was *more* serious than they originally thought.'

Here's one thing about Xfm; it has a long history of presenters getting themselves into trouble. Russell Brand was forced from the station for bringing homeless crack addicts into the studio who took drugs on air. *Breakfast Show* host Tom Binns received one of broadcast regulator Ofcom's all-time record fines of £50,000 for joking about bestiality during the school run. If there's one station that is used to dealing with big on-air problems, it's Xfm. I was sure their lawyers could take care of it and I could return to the topic of Christmas. However, their lawyers must have been burned out with all the cases they'd had to deal with over the years, because they wanted nothing to do with it. Never a good sign.

'You've got to report to Charing Cross Police Station tomorrow at 10 a.m., with a solicitor. And, they stressed, don't be late.'

So, as a little early Christmas present to myself, I hired a prohibitively expensive lawyer to defend a wholly spurious allegation against me (nothing's quite as festive as creeping down the stairs on Christmas Eve to find an invoice for £4,000, which is what he honestly cost, from a lawyer you spent just three hours with).

I turned up outside Charing Cross Police Station at 9.45 a.m. (see Chapter Twelve for the source of my warm feelings towards this place).

It was below freezing and I asked my lawyer, who was clearly enjoying his little Christmas bonus, what would happen once we got inside. 'Well, the first thing they'll probably do is arrest you.'

What? Arrest me? For making a joke on the radio? You've got to be kidding me. This never happens to Sandi Toksvig.

We passed through the imposing entrance, with me feeling agonisingly tense, braced and ready to be arrested. I looked around the reception (if that's the right word) and took in the kind of company I was keeping. Jobless, scruffy, pot smokers, not used to seeing daylight and with no real prospects in life – it was so nice to meet the listeners.

The two officers, a man and a woman, greeted me and told me that they were *not* going to arrest me, but that they were going 'to interview you under caution', which is basically one down. They led me to an interview room, which was just as you'd imagine (I'm making the assumption that you've never been arrested for perverting the course of justice, so this is all new to you): grey, drab and intimidating.

And I can't begin to tell you the degree to which these two officers radiated humourlessness.

'For the purposes of the tape,' said the fella in a voice that in other circumstances would seem like a lazy impression of a caricatured monotone policeman's voice, 'can you tell us about your radio show on Xfm?'

This was a *devastating* opening gambit.

If there was a book on how to hurt a professional presenter, then implying that you were entirely unfamiliar with their show would be the number one piece of advice.

Wounded, I explained what the show was like and told him about my mundane texts feature, knowing that this is what he was building up to.

He asked for an *example* of a mundane text.

In the context of that police interview room, this had now become quite the surreal conversation.

'Ok erm, how about this: "Dear Richard, my dog has died. From Steve."'

Silence. He leaned forward, raised his eyebrows and said, 'And that's meant to be funny, is it?' Now, I don't know about you, but this setting didn't strike me as a natural forum for dissecting comedy.

A seminar on a writing course, yes. A TV or radio commissioner's office, sure. But in a room built to extract confessions from horrible murderers? No.

I replied, 'Well, I er, don't think that material is designed to play these sorts of venues.'

The interview lasted two-and-three-quarter hours. Just reflect for a moment on that length of time for such a load of silliness.

I can't remember how they spun it out, but I'll always remember this: at one point the policeman played the 'offending broadcast' from a laptop.

Only he'd rewound it too far. So out of some tinny speakers on a chunky black HP laptop in the middle of a grim police interview room came Green Day's '*Basket Case*'. From the beginning. All of it.

So we had to sit there in silence – me, my lawyer, the female officer and the PC – listening to the whole three-and-a-half-minute song.

As it finally drew to an end, we reached the joke that brought me all the way from my house into police custody.

Amazingly, and I'd forgotten this, there was a line I'd added at the end. After the one about one man's liberty being dependent on how much the bloke on the jury liked emo I'd said, 'And if there are any policemen listening to this, please disregard everything I've just said.'

Now, considering our circumstances, that struck me as quite funny.

This, I thought, would be a wonderful opportunity to break the ice with the PC.

I smiled at him, gestured towards the laptop and said, 'Didn't you hear that?!'

His stony, motionless face just stared back at me. So ashen. So devoid of humour, this PC made those fellas on immigration at JFK look like Alan Carr.

At the end of our chat these officers told me they would be referring the matter to the CPS.

The CPS *kindly* left me hanging over Christmas, called me on 15 January and said that no further action would be taken. In that call, though, they sounded to me really rather embarrassed by the whole fiasco and asked me to 'never tell this story on the radio'.

And I gave them my word that I wouldn't.

And I haven't.

And this isn't the radio.

POSTSCRIPT

As I left the station, I saw the PC one last time, as he was climbing into his car, and I heard him exclaim, as he drove out of sight, 'Happy Christmas to all, and to all a good night!'[85]

With his Christmas message ringing in my ears, I realised that bygones will be bygones and walked home, having forgiven him for wasting my time with a spring in my step and love in my heart.[86]

---

[85] The PC didn't say these words; I just wanted to bring the essay back to the title of the chapter.

[86] Not true. I will *never* forgive him.

Chapter 22

I HOPE YOU DIE
BEFORE YOU GET OLD

Have you ever wondered if you're an Internet troll? Well, here's a simple test.

Question 1:
When you come across someone you don't particularly like on the TV or radio, what do you do?

(a) Turn over to something else
(b) Have a bit of a grumble about them with your friends
(c) Contact that person through Twitter to tell them you hope they die in a plane crash?

Question 2:

You notice on Twitter that Cher Lloyd is wishing happy birthday to her mother. What's the correct response?

(a) Feel touched at this display of the close ties between a mother and a daughter and tweet Cher to ask her to pass on your best wishes to her mum

(b) Do nothing

(c) Immediately contact Cher Lloyd to tell her to shut the fuck up or you'll kill her mother in front of her?

Question 3:

A teenager has died in tragic circumstances. How do you feel about this? Do you . . .

(a) Think 'There but for the grace of God . . .'

(b) Feel very sad for the family

(c) Feel very excited. You're about to have a right laugh posting 'jokes' of a sexual or violent nature on the Facebook tribute site set up in their memory (and not under your own name, under a made-up one)?

If you answered 'C' to any or all of those questions,

then congratulations! You're an Internet troll, and officially one of the country's most cowardly people.

Trolling is currently all the rage. It's this season's hottest form of anonymous abuse.

A bit like those boorish people who bang on about seeing Bowie above a pub in Derby before he made it, I remember through misty, rose-tinted spectacles the very earliest days – the embryonic, larval stage – of strange, lonely cranks threatening to kill television presenters online.

The Big Breakfast was one of the first TV programmes to have its own Internet forum, where viewers could share their considered thoughts with the wider *Big Breakfast*-viewing community.

I remember reading and watching as this chivalrous fellow defended Denise Van Outen against the terrible, monstrous slurs posted by another somewhat ill-mannered chap whose language wasn't best suited to genteel conversation: 'I wanna cut that bitch's head off', that kind of thing.

The two would go back and forth, page after page, unable to find common ground – the threats becoming more and more obscene, the defence rising up to protect Denise's honour more and more stridently.

I wanted to meet and extend a warm handshake of admiration to this valiant knight, rallying to my friend's aid.

But the police advised against this because when they looked into it, it turned out that both of them were the same person – just a single weirdo (and I imagine he was single), locked in a schizophrenic conversation with himself in perpetuity.

In hindsight, this man was a trailblazer for our present-day, spreading-like-the-Ebola-virus trolling community (although if he was around now, his old-fashioned, undeveloped levels of sexual menace would make him appear quaint).

But he *was* a near-perfect prototype for the upcoming generation of delusionals who violently overreact to people they see on the telly. Trolls of peeps on the telly and radio should hold that *Big Breakfast* forum man up as their Henry Ford (Henry Ford was believed by many to be an anti-Semite, something he has in common with a lot of trolls).

From that tiny split-personality acorn, a mighty oak of twats has grown.

Now, as a subject, trolling is slightly more complicated than it first appears.

Partly, this is because trolling is a broad church. The definition is not *entirely* settled. Or, at least, trolls will tell you it is not settled as a way of denying that they themselves are trolls.

But if there is one thing about this sorry business upon which we can all agree, then it is this: there is some strange and deformed alchemy that takes place when the ingredients include a keyboard, access to an online audience and relative anonymity.

I think it has brought out a side of human nature

that we haven't really seen before. At least not in this quantity.

Here's an experiment for you to try. Pop over to the *Daily Mail* online (*The Guardian* will also do the trick). This is important: choose the *most innocuous* celebrity story that you can find, the most inoffensive, the most banal.

Now take a look at the comments folk have left beneath.

Off you go. I'll be here waiting for you when you get back.

Welcome back.

Do you need to take a moment?

On the day I wrote this chapter, I nipped across to the *Daily Mail* online and the most humdrum showbizzy story I spotted was headlined, '*Sophie, Countess of Wessex, dishes up a feather hat for a day out with the Queen.*'

Just to sum the details of this story up for you, Prince Edward's wife had worn quite a big hat, with lots of feathers on it, while attending a celebratory event at Westminster Abbey. Despite being padded out for eight paragraphs, that really is your lot.

If you're now thinking to yourself something along these lines: 'Can't imagine anyone getting angry and spiteful about that. A hat, with some feathers on it, worn in a big church – what is there to say, really?'

Then, dear reader, you have a lot to learn about the world.

Dozens of people put finger to key (you know, like on

a keyboard. Looking at the word 'key' in that sentence, you might at first glance think it's incorrect, but it's not. I am right).

The correspondents put finger to key (see?), their energetic little digits stabbing angrily away, and they worked themselves into an apoplectic frenzy.

The third comment down comes from the otherwise perfectly even-tempered-sounding Vanessa and it reads, 'Just get rid of this disgusting family now.'

Another poster wrote of the Queen, who was standing beside the countess in the photo, 'She looks like an evil pink gremlin.'

Predominantly, the negative comments are about Kate Middleton – *who wasn't even there.*

Now, I don't know Vanessa, but I suspect that had she been at Westminster Abbey that day and Sophie Wessex had wandered over to shake her hand, Vanessa wouldn't have told her that her family was disgusting. She would have done a small curtsey and nervously mumbled 'Nice hat, ma'am.'

People who outwardly appear so affable, make the most extravagantly rude, and frequently dark comments the second they get the chance to show off on Internet forums.

In perfectly respectable detached houses, middle-aged ladies, members of Inner Wheel, just back from taking their Airedale for a bracing walk across the Fens, pour their husbands a pre-dinner sherry and settle down in front of the computer for an evening of posting on how

Jennifer Ellison should have her hands cut off.

My interest in the various facets of this world was piqued by a strange little fellow who decided to troll *me*.

He was very distressed that I had replaced Simon Mayo on BBC Radio 5 Live. One might say he became obsessive. Or he went crazy. I will accept both of those theories.

As with the man who targeted Denise Van Outen, I think he secretly loves me, but he has a very silly way of showing it. The sooner he faces up to the fact that I will never love him back, the better his life will be.

This not-so-youngster first tried to woo me by sending me a link to a 'fansite' he'd created called 'Richard Bacon Is a Cunt'.

This service provided an up-to-the-minute running commentary of the radio show and highlighted anything he perceived as a slip-up or mistake. If, for example, I couldn't recall if the actress Maxine Peake was coming in on the following Tuesday or the Wednesday, saying it was one or the other, then he'd pounce (bringing truth to power).

Perhaps slightly surprised that his nitpicking hadn't led to us going on a date, my troll went further and began fantasising about my dying in a plane crash or my body being mangled in a car wreck.

The amount of time he dedicated to the site was impressive. It was updated so frequently that no sane reader could keep up. Every couple of weeks, the author was producing a *War and Peace*-length commentary featuring a single character and a single motif – Richard

Bacon, and his hatred thereof. Although I was the main character, I could still only manage to wade through a couple of the hundreds of entries before starting to nod off. Even the sporadic threats of death began to bore me after a while.

But the more I ignored him, the more desperately he tried to catch my eye. Like a dumpy junior office worker who's been spurned by an attractive account executive, he started turning up with ever bigger and more elaborate bunches of flowers. Although, instead of flowers, he came with links to pages full of violent abuse he sent to my wife, Mum and friends.

I used this rejected suitor (who would have given the rest of his life just to touch the hem of my garment) as a way of looking into the world of online abuse for a documentary I made for BBC3 called *The Anti-Social Network*. This chap was my springboard into a stagnant and fetid pool.

The deeper I waded, the more I began to realise that the celebrity-baiting, itself frequently very dark, is only entry-level stuff.

At its most degenerate is the trolling of sites set up in memory of young people who have died in terrible circumstances.

Like owls to conservatory windows, these trolls are drawn to slam head first into whatever they perceive as weakness.

I'm talking about things like Facebook sites about severely disabled children, set up by the parents so that the rest of the family can keep an eye on their son's or daughter's medical progress. To a troll it is a good moment, no, an exciting moment, when they stumble across one of these. They can't wait to make 'jokes' about how they hope 'the little retard' dies soon (an actual quote I just found).

Sometimes they'll take a beloved family photo that's been put on a memorial site and alter it. Taking, for example, a school photograph of a young man who hanged himself and adding a noose to his neck and blood to his eyes, or sticking the face of a girl killed by a train on the front of Thomas the Tank Engine.

The only objective of this is to play to and amuse their troll mates, whom they've never met. Although in the course of my research I did come across a pair of trolls who'd got married, having met over their shared love of anonymous abuse, computer monitors and their dearest hope that Nicola from Girls Aloud will one day accidentally have sex with 'a monkey infected with Aids' (another actual quote).

In other contests these ridiculous people, with their undeveloped and pathetic sense of humour, perhaps deserve some sympathy. Anyone expressing a violent opinion is only revealing their own unhappiness. There's clearly *a lot* missing from their lives.

The trolls themselves, however, will typically argue there is *nothing* wrong with them.

I'll let you make your own mind up. One troll I met had posted a comment about having 'anal sex up a tree' with a teenager who had recently died in tragic circumstances.

Do you think this is:

(a) normal, or

(b) not normal

Regardless of what you said, it's not normal.

But the trolling community (and they do see themselves as members of a community, although they're constantly falling out with each other, like alcoholics in a park) will tell you that trolling is some form of satire.

No doubt Peter Cook, the godfather of satire – who wrote sketches like 'One Leg Too Few', who founded London's first satirical nightclub and whose influence paved the way for *That Was the Week That Was* – was indeed hoping that that golden path would one day lead to some idiot claiming to have had anal sex up a tree with a dead child.

After the documentary was broadcast, I was contacted by a number of trolls. Many of them decided that I was 'waging a war on free speech'.

I'm not. But I *am* calling *all of them* cowards.

If you've got a little 'joke' about kids that have killed themselves, that as some 'principle' you feel the need to post on a website that *you know* the family are going to see, then at least post it under your own name or, even better, if you really have got something that you feel it's worthwhile saying, go and say it to the family's faces. So they know who you are. That's a *much* better demonstration of free speech.

Because if there's one thing I noticed from many of the misspelled tweets sent to me by trolls (a large proportion of which used exclusively capital letters) it is that trolls get very confused by freedom of speech. They believe that freedom of speech means you are free to say anything about anyone on any platform at any time.

They argue that, as the law currently stands, nothing you say can be illegal, and that it's only online that people (like me, apparently) are trying to put restrictions in place on one of our hard-fought liberties.

I invited quite a lot of them to test out their theory by calling up a radio station, under their own name, and without foundation calling a local businessman a rapist.

There will always be a point where free speech clashes with a person's right to protect their reputation, or themselves from harassment.

Besides, trolls aren't even posting under their own names. So whose free speech are we meant to be protecting?

And what's the noble cause they're fighting for? The right to mock grieving families. It's hardly civil rights.

For a few weeks I received a lot of silly little threats from a lot of silly little people. One of them sent a link to my wife Rebecca about our newborn son saying, 'Wow, found such a cute photo of Arthur!' When she clicked on it, up came a photo of a dead baby covered in blood. Another joke that Peter Cook would have admired and been envious that he'd never had the bottle to crack.

As for the person who conducted that two-year infatuation with me, after I'd asked him to stop with the tweets and violent abuse through a number of civil channels, I ended up reporting him to the police.

As part of the documentary, an investigator discovered he was a forty-three-year-old man, which somehow makes it all the more heatbreaking that he's so in love with me.

The age difference alone means I have no interest in having a romantic relationship with you. I'm so sorry.

Chapter 23

I LOVE THE SMELL OF SOHO HOUSE IN THE MORNING

'Stand down!'

'At ease!'

'As you were!'

These are just three of the military catchphrases I use in everyday life.

'Richard, here's your Floradora.'

At ease, barman of excellent Soho cocktail venue Milk & Honey.'

'Mr Bacon, was it you who ordered the medium rare hanger steak?'

'It was, indeed. Stand down, waitress at tremendous meat venue Hix.'

When, in a conversation, I interject a joke that doesn't work, I paper over the cracks with 'As you were, everyone.' Try it. You might like it.

Let me stress, this is not some silly affectation. This is a hangover from my army days.

I served for three years. I was stationed in Worksop, North Nottinghamshire.

A couple of years ago I went out to Normandy for the sixty-fifth anniversary of the D-Day landings with a friend's charity. I met an elderly chap there in uniform, proudly displaying a chest full of medals. I noticed that he too was from Nottinghamshire. His name is William. He was a para and explained that in June 1944 he'd been dropped behind enemy lines to prepare the way for the Normandy invasion. An astoundingly dangerous mission, with a chillingly basic plan: 'We're just going to drop you on the Nazis' heads. See if you can kill them all. The rest of us will be there in a couple of days. Have a good one.'

I spoke with William directly after a ceremony of commemoration.

If you have never served you won't understand this, but something passed between us that day. In a way that it does, and only does, between two veterans. There exists an unspoken bond, an understanding that those who have worn British military fatigues know instinctively.

He was a para for eleven years. I was in the army bit of the Combined Cadet Force at Worksop College (the private school I went to), every other Monday afternoon.

Our service was separated by a span of fifty years, yet our army experiences were *strikingly* similar.

William was dropped behind enemy lines in Northern

France; I was dropped into the centre of Worksop, with some Kendal mint cake, a compass and a map, and ordered to find my way back to school. I didn't actually find my way back; they had to send out a search party, from which I hid.[87]

In the end I got thrown out of the Combined Cadet Force for constant minor infringements of their stupid rules. But the thing about being an army man is that it's hard to truly get out of your system.

Some years after my honorable discharge (my words, certainly not my school's), my presenting career took me to Sandhurst Military Academy. As a feature on that children's television show I used to work on, I was to take part in their famous Officer Training programme. A condensed version – the standard year's worth of officer training compacted into three weeks. This involved me moving into the barracks, running the assault courses, jumping into nuclear, chemical and biological suits in minutes, and completing the passing-out parade.

On the final day, as the tripod and camera were being folded into the boot of our estate car, one of the Sandhurst Military Academy senior brass invited me into his office. A quite majestic office. All oak panelling with grandiose portraits of renowned and intimidating-looking British military generals earnestly watching over us. I muttered

---

[87] Note to my school: it's deeply irresponsible to drop a public school boy in the centre of a rough town dressed in pretend army gear, complete with puttees and beret. I was essentially put in fancy dress and dropped a couple of minutes away from the local comp; they used to beat us up *even when we were in our regular clothes.*

some compliment about the place and he noticed me looking at the paintings.

'Richard,' he said, with a warmth his voice clearly wasn't used to. 'Look around you. These are the courageous men who have fought for Britain. Many of them took decisions on the battlefield which changed the entire course of history.'

He took a seat behind his desk, sitting so straight-backed it looked painful, and gestured to a few of them. I won't pretend that my recall is so sharp as to be able to recall the names of each of these historic figures, but I do remember the battles he mentioned included Waterloo, the Charge of the Light Brigade and the Boer War.[88]

At this point I felt fairly comfortable, assuming he was simply giving me a bit of a history lesson.

'Let me get to the point,' he said next. 'I've been very impressed by what I've seen from you. I think you are officer material, and so do my colleagues. We'd like you to do this for real. We'd like you to at least *consider* leaving your current job . . . and joining the British army.'

He smiled a smile his face clearly wasn't used to and

---

[88] Years later, it struck me that the Charge of the Light Brigade probably wasn't the best example of the decision-making power of the British army's leaders (in one of the first references to come up when you search online, it's described as 'one of the most gallant, idiotic and futile examples of British military incompetence', and *The Times* of the day called it 'an atrocity without parallel'), but he *definitely* mentioned it in his list. In fairness, at no point did he say he was talking about *good* decisions made by generals, just decisions which changed history, so technically you can't argue with his choice. If that senior brass chappie is reading this and he's thinking of doing this speech again, here's a bit of advice: next time, when you mention the Boer War and Crimea, also reference World War II. That was a much clearer victory for the British.

added 'and who knows? Maybe one day you'll find yourself on one of these walls.'

Wow.

Well, that's quite an offer.

Made in a most enticing venue.

By a persuasive and inspiring man.

And when the offer was put before me like that – to fight for Her Majesty and the citizens of this realm, to potentially lay down my life to protect the national interest; to do an Englishman's duty – there was only one answer.

Are you mad?

He'd misinterpreted the situation entirely. He thought I had coped with everything they threw at me because I was a natural soldier.

I'm the antithesis of a natural soldier.

I don't like guns.

I don't like knives.

I don't like being shouted at.

I don't like combat gear.

I don't like getting up early.

I don't like killing people.

I don't like being killed.

And the only reason I had coped is because I knew it was so temporary.

I knew it didn't really matter if I couldn't make it over a wall.

I knew my inability to strip a rifle in fifty-five seconds would never be a genuine stumbling block in my life.

And I knew when those three weeks were over, I could get back to London where I had Sky TV, overpriced members' clubs and wouldn't have to request an exeat (which would most likely be denied anyway) whenever I wanted to leave my house.

I told him thanks a lot – but he had to realise: *I'm on the telly*. It's a doss. And never does anyone get shot in the stomach.[89]

And besides, I thought to myself, I didn't want to be next to the duke of Wellington or the brave Lord Cardigan[90] on the oak wall of an august Sandhurst Military Academy office wall. I wanted to be next to Mark Curry, on a wall at the entrance to the *Blue Peter* garden at BBC Television Centre (which I achieved. Tragically, the immortality I thought this represented was short-lived because they moved the ruddy garden up to Salford and sold TVC off for flats. I'm guessing that Wellington's still there).

As I bid that military man good day (seemed like the right turn of phrase), I thought about how I was going tea picking in Darjeeling the following week, and was then off to do some filming in LA. I was hardly going to turn that down in exchange for a seven-month stint avoiding sniper fire in Bosnia.

I wasn't rude. It would be an excellent opportunity for

---

[89] Tim Westwood is the exception to that rule. And yes, he did do TV, you've forgotten about MTV's *Pimp My Ride UK*.

[90] I should point out that Lord Cardigan's wrong decision led to the deaths of over five hundred soldiers, whereas mine simply killed one contract. In the aftermath of his shame, I wouldn't be surprised if Talksport offered Lord Cardigan the *Breakfast Show* too (provided he cleared their sexism levels stress test – but, as a nineteenth-century figure, who worked exclusively with men and rarely came into contact with women, I imagine he'd just scrape it).

someone else. I told him that I was flattered.

But I made it clear that I would never, under any circumstances, leave my job.

(One month later, I left my job.)

Chapter 24

GOODBYE DENIM

As I write, I am in the final month of the 16–34 demographic.

At the stroke of midnight as the 29th turns into the 30th November, I will become an irrelevance to most advertisers. I shall no longer be welcome in Falaraki. BBC3 won't care for my custom. And *Hollyoaks* will, in an instant, become even less appealing than it already is.

For most folk, birthday milestones are all about turning 18, 21, 30 and 40. But not me. This is honestly the one I've been dreading the most.

The day you turn 35 is the day when you are officially no longer a young person.

For as long as you're safely ensconced inside that 16–34 demo, even its latter stages, you could still feasibly have sex with Effy from Skins without being considered pathetic.

And what is the next demographic band anyway? 35 to what? 50? 60? I don't want to be grouped together with a load of people who can remember Apollo 13. Not the film. The actual incident.

People have often asked why Jesus gave His life when He did. I know why. He simply wasn't prepared to suffer the indignity of continuing life outside that most revered of demographics.

Sure, he'd still be able to turn water into wine, but he would not be able to drink it in the Hawley Arms in Camden.

BTW, I've seen images of Jesus – stained-glass windows, religious texts, crisps – He was a terrible 33. He looked, at best, like a rough 58. Let me point you in the direction of a miracle Jesus. Touche Eclat.

Anyway, unlike Jesus, I'm not taking the coward's way out. I will suffer in silence at the knowledge that if I go to a Florence gig people there will assume I'm a dad looking for his daughter who's missed her curfew. I'll know that when Jonathan Ive designs the next Apple product, he won't have my three-and-a-half-decade-old fingers in mind, and that if I die, then from 12.01 a.m. on November 30th onwards no one will say, 'He died tragically young.' They'll just say, 'Richard died.'

So goodbye 16–34s. I won't be a member of your gang anymore. I'll be leaving you to your downloaded episodes of *Two Pints of Lager and a Packet of Crisps* and your 'Judge Jules Back to Ibiza' CDs. Your city-centre nights out and the downing of vodka jelly shots in Ha-Ha Bar. Your skinny jeans and your chlamydia. Your high risk of dying in an RTA or a motiveless stabbing. I'm off to enjoy a full eight hours' sleep, some decent wine and dinner at the Ivy. Fuck you.